D0891569

The Mind of William Paley

Portrait of William Paley
by G. Romney © the National Portrait Gallery, London.

The Mind
of
William Paley

A Philosopher and His Age

D. L. LeMahieu

UNIVERSITY OF NEBRASKA PRESS
LINCOLN AND LONDON

*The publication of this book was assisted by a grant from
The Andrew W. Mellon Foundation.*

Library of Congress Cataloging in Publication Data

LeMahieu, D L 1945–
     The mind of William Paley.

     Based on the author's thesis, Harvard University.
     Bibliography: p.
     Includes index.
     1. Natural theology—History of doctrines. 2. Paley, William,
1743–1805. Natural theology. 3. Paley, William, 1743–1805. I. Title.
BL182.L45   230'.3'0924   75-22547
ISBN 0-8032-0865-0

To
Lloyd F. LeMahieu
and
Ruth J. LeMahieu

CONTENTS

PREFACE

IN THE PREFACE TO HIS FINAL AND MOST MAJESTIC
publication—the *Natural Theology,* published in 1802—
William Paley wrote that the "following discussion alone
was wanted to make up my works into a system; . . . the
public have now before them the evidences of Natural
Religion, the evidences of Revealed Religion, and an account of the duties that result from both."[1] It is the intention of the present book to analyze that system, the personal influences and intellectual traditions which shaped
it, and its impact on the nineteenth century.

Paley merits study for two reasons. First, in both his
theological and political works, he asked questions which
often dig at the core of philosophy: questions such as
whether the tools of human reason could demonstrate the
existence of God and, if so, reveal something comprehensible about his mysterious nature; whether the Bible was a
reliable historical document or simply a clever forgery
which had deceived gullible men; whether a just society
was possible in a world of self-interested individuals.

He answered these questions with a thoroughness and
lucidity rare in eighteenth-century divines. His statement
of the teleological argument for the existence of God
remains one of the clearest and most comprehensive in
all philosophy. He is more consistent than Cicero, more
thorough than Aquinas, more concise than any of his con-

temporary theologians. Moreover, his rational proofs for the credibility of the Gospel in *Horae Paulinae* and *Evidences of Christianity* are masterpieces of logical exposition. Paley never wasted words. His *Principles of Moral and Political Philosophy* distills, in one volume, influences from two centuries of social and political thought and earned the praise of John Maynard Keynes, who called it "an immortal book."[2]

But there is another reason why Paley deserves scrutiny. In politics and theology, he stands at the climax of an intellectual tradition which, though repudiated by some and modified by others, lasted long into the nineteenth century. His *Principles*—to quote Keynes again—"was for a generation or more an intellectual influence on Cambridge only second to Newton."[3] And his *Natural Theology*—the centerpiece of his entire philosophic system—spawned a mass of literature on natural religion which culminated in the famous Bridgewater Treatises. No mere sidelight to the vast spectacle of eighteenth-century British thought, Paley was a dynamic transmitter of some of its most cherished assumptions. It was Paley to whom hundreds of intellectuals turned for guidance on significant philosophic matters and whose works the universities adopted as textbooks for a generation of students which included Thomas Arnold and Charles Darwin. "I took in the whole argument," wrote the aging Cardinal Manning in reference to his reading of the *Evidences* at college, "and I thank God that nothing has ever shaken it."[4]

In the same preface where Paley asserted that his works formed a unified and coherent whole, he also admitted that "they have been written in an order the very reverse of that in which they ought to be read."[5] After an analysis of Paley's life and an examination of the questions which provoked his thought, the present study will treat his works in the order "in which they ought to be read"; it will argue that the argument from design, or the teleological argument for the existence of God—the terms were used interchangeably in the Enlightenment—exercised a powerful dominion over the thinking of not only Paley, but also many of the British intellectuals who preceded him. Paley invigorated and reinforced an important tradition in British thought.

I should be happy to express my gratitude to a number of people and institutions. H. J. Hanham and John Clive advised and aided me when an earlier draft of this study was a doctoral dissertation at Harvard University. My friends James Wilkinson of Harvard and John Schneider of the University of Nebraska read the entire manuscript without complaint and offered valuable suggestions for its improvement. I owe a special debt to W. R. Carr of the University of Wisconsin, whose perceptive and exhaustive critique of this study saved me from many errors, major and minor. I am grateful also to Frederick Luebke, Robert Sullivan, Thomas Moodie, and Arthur Zilversmit for help along the way.

I received much assistance from library staffs at Harvard, the British Museum, Cambridge, Oxford, Dr. William's Library, and the University of London. Also, at various stages my work has been eased by grants from Harvard and Lake Forest College.

Finally, my greatest debt is to those acknowledged in the dedication. It has been my fortune to have these good people as parents.

The Mind of William Paley

CHAPTER 1

Portrait of a Theologian

THREE ENVIRONMENTS SHAPED THE MIND OF WILLIAM
Paley, each offering its own particular contribution to the
development of his intellect. Born in Yorkshire, he retained the simple, almost bucolic manner of a North
Countryman throughout his life, charming his acquaintances with his pungent wit and concealing in his informality a penetrating, analytic mind. Following his
fifteenth birthday, he spent most of the next two decades
at Cambridge, where he first demonstrated his proficiency
in mathematics as an undergraduate and then, as a fellow
and lecturer, mastered a century of moral and theological
thought to become one of the university's finest teachers.
Here, too, he involved himself with a group of friends
anxious to reform both Cambridge and the Church, friends
whose philosophic outlook he shared and whose biases
he inherited when he later committed to print the substance of his lectures.

Finally, it was as a clergyman in the environment of the
Church that he returned to the North, devoting the remainder of his sixty-two years to his clerical duties, his
family, and his writing. It was here that he composed
hundreds of sermons which served as the basis of his later
religious works, and also revealed a piety and commitment to traditional Christian dogma often hidden from his
published writings. It was here also during the turbulent

1790s that he abandoned some of his earlier, more flexible political views for the precise and often legalistic inquiries into the credibility of the Gospels and the intricacies of teleology. Each of these environments—Yorkshire, Cambridge, and the Church—played a critical role in forming the mind Leslie Stephen praised for its "admirable lucidity" and "shrewd sense." Each requires further exploration.[1]

As a man who attained a degree of esteem in his later life unparalleled by any other living ecclesiastic, Paley was fortunate in his early biographers. George Wilson Meadley, his friend and close companion during his last years in Bishop-Wearmouth, gathered together both factual information about his youth and a series of fascinating personal evaluations by his university friends. Meadley's *Memoirs of William Paley,* published four years after Paley's death, went through a number of editions and served as the basis for Edmund Paley's biography, prefaced to the complete works published in 1825.[2] Using family records and personal recollections unavailable to Meadley, Edmund composed a larger, more complete biography of his father that gained in thoroughness what it lacked in compression and style. Both Meadley and the younger Paley confronted a similar problem, however; the life of Paley was an eminently undramatic affair, rarely punctuated by incidents that might capture the imagination of a sympathetic and creative biographer. He read, studied, and reflected upon some of the most fundamental questions of human existence and offered in his works the testament of his daily preoccupations.

II

William Paley was born in Peterborough in July, 1743, and was baptized in the cathedral one month later. His father, also named William, had been a sizar at Christ's

College, Cambridge, where he took his degree in 1734. Shortly thereafter he was installed as vicar of Helpstone, Northamptonshire, a post which paid £30 a year "plus flower seeds." A few years later he gained a stall at Peterborough, where, in 1742, he married Elizabeth Clapham, a woman of moderate wealth and position who at one time considered the marriage "beneath her." In 1745, when their first son was two years old, the Paleys moved to Giggleswick, Yorkshire, where the elder Paley had been appointed headmaster of the grammar school. Here he would remain for the rest of his life.[3]

Paley's parents were thrifty and parsimonious, always worried about a recent expense that might have been spared. Mrs. Paley, a small, "keen-eyed" woman of great intelligence, so successfully cultivated a £400 dowry that at her death it had become a £2,200 bequest to her family. Her husband, whose salary as headmaster began at a paltry £80 per year, eventually accumulated as the result of meticulous saving and shrewd investment a fortune of well over £7,000. "Take care of thy money lad," he told his son before the younger Paley left home.[4]

As a boy, Paley was awkward, uncoordinated, and physically unable to participate in the youthful athletics that so often determine a child's popularity and self-esteem. Subjected to "the taunts and jeers of his companions," he nevertheless developed an effective and engaging weapon with which to counter the jests of his peers; he became a comic, a wit who gained through laughter what he could not achieve by physical prowess. "A man who is not sometimes the fool," he later explained, "is always one."[5]

Both of these two facts—an upbringing by frugal parents and the youthful genesis of a penetrating wit—would in themselves be unremarkable, were it not for their lasting influence on Paley's thought and character. The child whose uncle once separated, grain by grain, two pounds of salt and pepper in order to save a few farthings would eventually become the Cambridge don who refused to sign the petition for relief of subscription to the Thirty-nine Articles because he "could not afford to keep a conscience." The youth whose father converted an obscure post as headmaster into a financially successful vocation would eventually become the clerical pluralist who garnered one of the most lucrative rectories in England, that of Bishop-Wearmouth, valued at £1,200 a year.

More important, he would become the ethicist who defined virtue as "the doing good to mankind, for the sake of everlasting happiness"—a definition which scores of nineteenth-century critics condemned as the morality of barter and the ethics of the marketplace. Of course there was nothing unusual about an eighteenth-century moral philosopher defending the sanctity of pecuniary values —and through his life Paley retained the possessive individualism instilled in him at youth—but his case is complicated somewhat by another trait, also acquired early on, which often implicitly challenged conventional norms and mores.

In the chemistry of Paley's famed wit and informal manner, there always remained the critical element of the unexpected; he gloried in acting or responding in precisely the opposite manner to that which others anticipated. Thus, when a certain minor writer named Henry Digby Best first met him in the late 1790s, Paley was neither the person, nor the philosopher he expected. "A thick, short, square-built man" with a countenance marked by "bushy brows, a snub nose, and projecting teeth," Paley struck the earnest Best as an essentially "ugly" creature who, not disdaining to enliven his conversation with "vulgar" phrases, discussed only the most common things in a frankly common manner. Once, while seated in a small rush-bottomed chair, Paley suddenly rose, impatiently thrusting it away from him: "I hate these nasty little chairs," he exclaimed in his broad Yorkshire accent, "they sink in the middle and *throost one's goots* up into one's *brains*." At dinner he talked only of "the pork *staakes*" and when asked specific questions about his philosophy by the shaken Best, generally replied with a humorous anecdote followed by a hearty laugh. To Best, Paley "never seemed to care seriously about any thing" and this flippancy, combined with his rural informality, "weakened that splendour of his literary reputation."[6]

As a teacher, he often challenged the assumptions of his students, himself advocating a position so extreme, so bordering on the ludicrous, that the students were forced to clarify their own stand in relation to it. The most famous illustration of this method occurred in his *Principles* when he compared English mercantile society to a flock of pigeons who viciously horded grain solely for the pleasure of "the feeblest and worst of the whole set, a child, a woman, a madman, or a fool."[7] Although in the ensuing chapters Paley retraced his steps and eventually justified virtually every abuse the "pigeon analogy" satirized, its inclusion baffled many of his readers and probably resulted in serious harm to his career. Yet, though many mistakenly accepted it as his final position, one of its functions was simply to startle and amuse his audience into a recognition of their own values.

Since Paley often directed his satiric barbs against himself, his wit possessed another, more obvious dimension. It transformed what might have been personal defects—his accent, dress, and manner—into charming and engaging assets. His countrified attitudes and interests became one of his most outstanding personal characteristics. "I will tell you in what consists the *summum bonum* of human life," he once said; "it consists in reading Tristram Shandy, in blowing with a pair of bellows into your shoes in hot weather, and roasting potatoes under the grate in cold weather."⁸ The Yorkshire soil that nurtured him thus sustained him throughout his life.

On 16 November 1758, Paley's father enrolled him in Christ's College, Cambridge, even though he did not take up residence until the following year.⁹ Such residence was not required and, more important, the young Paley lacked the background in mathematics which the university required. Giggleswick had prepared him well enough in classics, but the decalogues of Livy and the elegies of Virgil were little help when it came to the exploration of Euclidean geometry and Newtonian physics.¹⁰ Ironically, it was the northern schools which generally sent up the best-coached mathematics students,¹¹ and so, with the financial aid of his father, Paley spent most of 1758 in Dishforth, where he was taught by a private tutor. In October of 1759 he finally entered Christ's College, the college of Milton, and embarked on a crucial phase of his career.

III

Cambridge University in the mid-eighteenth century was at the nadir of its long history. The undergraduates, sharply divided into classes based on tuition fees and social standing, immersed themselves in the pleasurable diversions of the good life: they conversed; they drank; they traveled extensively during the long vacations. The professors, who rarely lectured, often knew little of their subjects and regarded their offices as sinecures. The libraries lacked catalogues and in some cases had misplaced most of their books. About the only challenge thrust upon undergraduates was provided by the final examinations in the third year, and even those depended upon the quality and integrity of the moderators.¹²

Yet, the decadence of Cambridge can easily be exaggerated. For the student who was seriously dedicated to scholarly inquiry, a good education was still possible, provided he attached himself to an interested tutor and scrupulously avoided most of the entertaining diversions. Paley probably lacked the funds to indulge in the more picturesque activities enjoyed by his more affluent fellow students, though there is some indication that in his first two years he devoted little time to study. At the beginning of his third year, however, he made a happy choice of teachers in John Wilson, a tutor famed for his ability to prepare examination students in the critical subject of mathematics. Enlisting the aid of another excellent adviser, Wilson drilled Paley to a high point of readiness.[13]

The major part of the Cambridge examination was called Acts and Opponencies, an exercise in which the candidate would argue a series of questions with three other undergraduates chosen by the moderators. On each of three questions, or Acts, the examinee confronted a different undergraduate opponent. Naturally, the questions varied in difficulty, and regrettably few students mastered Latin sufficiently to use the required syllogistic logic.[14] Prior to the examinations, undergraduates were granted special privileges such as not attending morning chapel to allow them more time for study. The examinations were conducted in public and often in an atmosphere of intense drama.

For his Act in natural philosophy, Paley chose to argue *"Aeternitas poenarum contradicit divinis attributis,"* that is, against the eternity of hell's torments. This choice stirred a minor controversy since it was customary for the opponent to defend the worst side of any question. In requesting to argue against the orthodox position, Paley provoked the Master of Christ's, Hugh Thomas, to intervene. One evening shortly before the examination, Paley rushed "in great fright" to the rooms of his chief moderator, Richard Watson, and informed him that Thomas was "afraid of being looked upon as a heretic at Lambeth" and would not permit the examination to continue. Watson, who prided himself on "never refraining a question for debate," nevertheless decided to place a *"non"* before the *"contradicit,"* thereby settling the issue.[15]

On 10 October 1762, Paley appeared at the Senate House, with "his hair full-dressed, a deep ruffled shirt, and new silk stockings, which aided by his gestures, his actions, and his whole manner . . . excited no small mirth among his spectators."[16] Yet those who came to laugh stayed to cheer; Paley annihilated his opponents, including a third-year man from Norwich who had been promised a thousand pounds were he to achieve the highest honors. In June of 1763, Paley graduated as Senior Wrangler, the highest distinction Cambridge bestowed upon an undergraduate.[17]

In his Acts and Opponencies, Paley had revealed a talent for mathematics that would have important repercussions in the form, method, and purpose of his later thought. In Euclidean geometry, the reasoner begins with relatively few theorems and argues according to a prescribed logic to a new set of truths that are as clear, distinct, and infallible as his original premises. The entire system is closed, self-contained, and certain. There are no variables that cannot either be measured or deduced, once the reasoner grants the initial assumptions; in geometry, intellectual hypocrisy becomes an impossibility. The strength and weakness of the entire system, however, rests on the very abstractness of its demonstrations; its conclusions embody no authentic metaphysical validity outside the reality they attempt to describe.

Though Paley quite properly considered himself an empiricist rather than a rationalist, his philosophy always retained a geometrical bent. In the *Principles*, for example, he began with a series of "Preliminary Considerations," or propositions concerning the principle of utility, and from them deduced in the following chapters the duties of men to themselves, their families, and their society. More sig-

nificant perhaps, the whole tone of his argument suggested
the self-enclosed certainty of a Euclidean demonstration;
"if such a proposition is true," he continually seemed to
say, "then the following conclusions must also be true."
This air of inevitability in his method of reasoning per-
meated almost all his prose. It bestowed upon it the appearance of close argument, while at the same time
prompting a vague uneasiness as to the value and depth of
what was being claimed.

Shortly after he had taken his degree, Paley, only twenty
and still too young to be offered a fellowship, secured a
position at a Greenwich academy that was particularly
designed for students who sought military careers. Here he
taught Latin, but the drudgery and harshness of the school,
combined with his lack of interest in the subject, soon
made the experience intensely disagreeable. "The room
stank of piss," he would vividly recall later on, "and a little
boy came up, as soon as I was seated, and began—b,a,b,
bab; b.l.e. ble; babble."[18] After a bitter disagreement with
the headmaster, he resigned and became a junior curate in
a Greenwich church. Yet, this position also proved un-
fulfilling, "for he reckoned that it was bad enough to be a
simple rat, as was his cant term for curate, but to be the rat
of rats"—or second curate—he could not endure.[19]

Alone and seemingly with few prospects, he carefully
wrote out in English and then translated into Latin an
essay, "*Utrum civitati perniciosior sit Epicuri an Zenonis
philosophia*," which he submitted 1765 for the Member's Prize at Cambridge. In it, he again attempted to
defend an unpopular position. He championed Epicur-
ean morality because, in his view, a life of moderated
pleasure was more acceptable to the common man than
the strict asceticism of the Stoics, whom he dubbed "those
Pharisees in philosophy." He was quick, however, to
qualify his support for the Epicureans: "The intent of this
inquiry is not so much to defend the principles of either

sect, as to prove the insufficiency of both. For neither the welfare of the public is promoted, nor the happiness of the individual secured by either."[20] This critique of the ancient moralists, which revealed a nascent utilitarianism that eventually came to fruition in his *Principles*, won for Paley the Member's Prize and election to a fellowship at Christ's.

When Paley assumed his new position in the autumn of 1766, he could have chosen a life of leisure; Cambridge demanded virtually nothing of its fellows and most led dull, hollow lives.[21] He took his appointment seriously, however, and in 1768 was selected with John Law as an assistant to Anthony Shepard, his college tutor. Law taught mathematics while Paley lectured on metaphysics, moral philosophy, and, later, the Greek Testament. It was from these lectures that Paley rapidly gained a reputation as one of Cambridge's great teachers. One of his most famous students, William Frend, later recalled:

> . . . in the most familiar manner he discussed some subject in Locke or Clarke, or in moral Philosophy, pointing out the passages which we were to read for the next lecture day, and explaining everything in such a manner that the driest subjects were made interesting. At this time we were most of us employed in taking notes, and the manuscripts thus taken out of his lectures were not only in the highest repute in our own, but were eagerly sought after in other colleges.[22]

Paley's classroom notes, now preserved in the British Museum,[23] reveal that he based an enormous amount of his later philosophy on these Cambridge lectures. The debt was most pronounced in his ethical and political thought. The organization of the *Principles* corresponded almost exactly to the outline of his lectures; in both, he began with general observations on the nature of ethics, then proceeded directly into considerations of particular obligations such as the responsibilities of marriage, the nature of contracts, and the evils of fornication and drunkenness.[24] By 1773, he had already defined virtue as "the doing good to mankind in obedience to the will of God and for the sake of everlasting happiness," and viewed most moral behavior as the product of habit rather than contemplation. His lectures also included the famous pigeon analogy which later provoked so much controversy.[25] Though he continued throughout his life to ruminate on the subjects he taught as a fellow, it would not be unfair to Paley's later achievement to assert that his intellectual system was firmly cast by the time he reached his thirtieth birthday.

Critical to the formation of this system was Paley's involvement in a small intellectual circle of Cambridge Latitudinarians known as the Hyson Club. Formed in 1757 "for the purpose of rational conversation," the Hyson Club held no regular meetings, nor bound itself to any particular topic of discussion. Instead, it consisted of a loosely knit group of academics who met occasionally to exchange witticisms and opinions about current topics of interest. The Hyson Club had its personal rivalries and misunderstandings, but generally it encouraged the development of solid friendships in a polite, intellectual atmosphere.[26]

Paley joined the Hyson Club shortly after becoming a fellow and first became acquainted there with some of his closest friends. One of these was John Law, Paley's associate under Anthony Shepard. Born in Cumberland in 1745, Law attended Charterhouse School and then Christ's College, where he was Second Wrangler in 1766. Though he had not known Paley as an undergraduate, as fellows they shared living accommodations, attended the London theater together, and traveled throughout England during the long vacations. Considered by Boswell a man of "uncommon genius," Law formed a lifelong friendship with Paley that involved a constant interchange of letters and visits, extending long after Law was elevated to the Bishopric of Killala in 1787.[27] It would be through this friend that Paley made one of his most important acquaintances.

When Paley met John Law's father, Edmund Law was master of Peterhouse and Knightsbridge Professor of Moral Philosophy.[28] The elder Law's years at Cambridge had been laden with frustration: in 1756, the Duke of Newcastle had denied him the deanship of Ely;[29] four years later his appointment as head librarian was almost blocked by "Dr. Walker's proposal to sink the office . . . and apply the profits to his Botanical Garden."[30] He seemed "not a little eager" for the Lady Margaret Professorship of Divinity in 1764, but lost it to Zachary Brooke, who never lectured.[31] In 1769, at the age of sixty-six, he finally attained a position of influence, the bishopric of Carlisle.

Another older man at Cambridge was also to have an important influence on Paley. In 1754 the dynamic and brilliant John Jebb entered Peterhouse, where, despite a series of withering illnesses, he distinguished himself by his ability in languages and mathematics. He won the Latin prose award in 1758 and three years later became a fellow. He was a comoderator on Paley's examination and maintained a close relationship with him for a decade to come. A man of rare courage and persistence, Jebb suffered a number of personal setbacks at Cambridge; in 1768 he sought the professorship of Arabic but lost out to Samuel Halifax, who, unlike Jebb, knew nothing of the language and regarded the post as a sinecure. When Halifax moved to the professorship of civil law in 1770, Jebb again applied for the position and again lost. The reason lay in his personality and his political views. In 1764, he supported the losing candidate for an influential university office; in 1768, his private lectures on the Greek Testament so enraged college officials that they forbade students to attend them; a year later he declared himself in opposition to the Tory party and, with one other rebel, voted against the address of loyalty to George III.³² Like many other members of the Hyson Club, Jebb was an outsider.

Yet he was sincerely interested in the welfare of the university. For some time, the Cambridge examination system had aroused the indignation of its most dedicated teachers. Students faced no examinations in their first two years and what they did confront in the third year was narrowly conceived and inadequately administered. Worse, some noblemen and fellow commoners were never tested at all. Jebb decided to act. In 1774, he composed a nineteen-article plan for change and, with the aid of Richard Watson, rallied the reformers.³³

A brilliant and disciplined undergraduate, Watson had been Second Wrangler in 1759, and was shortly thereafter elected to a fellowship. In 1764, he was appointed professor of chemistry, though he confessed he "had never read a syllable on the subject, nor seen a single experiment in it."³⁴ Nevertheless, after fourteen months of intensive reading and preparation, he emerged to give a lecture series that received the acclaim of his undergraduates and eventually earned him election to the Royal Society. When Thomas Rutherforth died in 1771, vacating the Regius Professorship of Divinity, Watson applied for and captured the coveted post. Again he mastered a new field and again established himself as an authority in it. This diligence and deep earnestness made him a natural ally to Jebb in the struggle for higher academic standards.

Jebb and Watson received support from the Hyson Club and from various colleges in the university. At Christ's, Paley offered continuing encouragement and active support, signing the various petitions and voting with the reformers in the Senate. The main opposition centered at St. John's, where the master, William Samuel Powell, ruled with absolute authority. Ironically, Powell had initiated in 1765 a series of annual examinations at St. John's

which vastly improved the quality of the college and
served as Jebb's model for reforming the entire university.
But Powell did not want to share his creation; he was "by
nature positive and obstinate and never to be out of what
he had once got into his head."[35] Powell detested Jebb and
fought academic reform with persistence, bitterness, and,
to the dismay of the reformers, success.

Every proposal put forward by the reformers lost, once
by the heartbreaking margin of one vote. Immediately
after one plan suffered defeat, Jebb would draft another,
more moderate version to appease the conservatives. But
nothing worked. Some were lost in the preliminary stages;
others survived only to be killed after debate in the Senate.
The struggle continued intermittently until 1775, when
Jebb broke with the established church and became a
Unitarian. Discredited by this precipitous action, the
movement dissolved.[36]

Thus, during a critical period in the formation of Paley's
intellect, his closest associations were with scholars and
teachers genuinely interested in molding Cambridge into
something more than a finishing school for the social elite.
Moreover, the acute concern for teaching and education
which Paley shared with his colleagues in the Hyson Club
was directly related to another characteristic of this unusual group: Watson, Paley, the Laws, and John Jebb were
all Latitudinarians whose later speculations in politics and
theology, though too diverse and idiosyncratic to be clas-
sified as Paley's "school" (as Leslie Stephen asserted),[37]
possessed a coherence and unity of purpose that indicate
strong ties of sympathy and collaboration during their
years together at Cambridge.

First, all were sturdy advocates of a religion grounded
upon the teleological argument for the existence of God;
that is, a religion based on empirical testimony and subject
to the scrutiny of a disinterested reason. Thus, for example,
in his *Lectures on Divinity* published in 1796 when he was
Norrison Professor, John Hey initiated his analysis with a

panegyric to the "unity of design" that pervaded the universe and proclaimed God's glory, wonder, and power. Later in the same book, he argued that, as a concomitant to this design, "our immediate concern is *proving* the Books of the New Testament." Although Paley himself would write the central texts of these two interrelated creeds, they also lay behind Edmund Law's somewhat muddled theory of progress in *Considerations on the Theory of Religion* and John Jebb's fervent repudiation of Trinitarian dogma.[38]

In at least some of their later publications, members of the Hyson Club also shared a belief in the fundamental tenets of theological utilitarianism. Law wrote favorably of John Gay's utilitarian definition of virtue—later adapted by Paley—and Richard Watson, whose liberal attitudes would condemn him to remain Bishop of Llandaff longer than any other man in British history, argued in one of his tracts that "there is not a single precept in the Gospel . . . which is not calculated to promote our happiness."[39]

Finally—and this was perhaps the most characteristic attitude of the entire group—the Cambridge Latitudinarians maintained that, in Watson's words, "free disquisition is the best means of illustrating the doctrine and establishing the truth of Christianity."[40] This belief in tolerance, in promoting rational inquiry by creating an open marketplace of ideas, was, as in the case of the deists earlier in the century, obviously a matter of self-interest. Men like Watson demanded a climate of understanding if they were to survive and advance in the ecclesiastical hierarchy. But their advocacy of this notion also sprang from deeper roots. "Unable to make the peasants about me good Protestants," John Law wrote as Bishop of Killala in 1787, "I wish to make them good Catholics, good citizens, good anything."[41] This pragmatic, tolerant attitude toward religious dogma, so pervasive in the lives and writings of the Cambridge reformers, ultimately derived from a profound

veneration for the dignity of men and of ideas; to promote
the happiness of society, each person must be permitted to
shape his own ideology and destiny.

For the Hyson Club, the most dramatic opportunity to
test these principles occurred during the protracted
struggle for the relief from subscription to the Thirty-nine
Articles. The debate over subscription began innocently
enough in June of 1757 when in a "Sermon before the
University of Cambridge, in defence of Subscription . . ."
William Samuel Powell maintained that the Articles were
a real and proper test of religious uniformity. Taking
exception to this stand, Archdeacon Francis Blackburne of
Cleveland asserted in a series of pamphlets that the Articles were not consistent with Scripture and thus posed a
false standard of man's religious faith.[42] In close collaboration with Edmund Law, Blackburne refined his position
and in 1766 published his definitive statement, *The Confessional.* Invoking the principle that the Scriptures "contain all things necessary to salvation and are the sole
ground of the faith of a Christian," he argued that

> all imposed subscriptions to articles of faith, and religious
> doctrine, conceived in unscriptural terms and enforced by
> human authority, are utterly unwarrantable, and not to be
> defended by arguments and pretences, highly dishonorable to
> the sacred writings and, in many cases, contrary to the ex-
> press content of them.[43]

This conclusion sent the orthodox rushing to their ink-
wells; in more than a score of pamphlets, indignant divines poured a stream of abuse on Blackburne and his
ideas.[44]

One of these was Thomas Rutherforth, whose "Vindication of the Right . . . to Subscribe," published in 1766,
warned against "false teachers" such as Blackburne. When
this pamphlet was answered by one Benjamin Dawson,
Rutherforth again took to the press, this time publishing an

even more bitter attack on the reformers. As a deep, often unfair adversary, he inevitably provoked indignation from those he challenged. "Hath he not attacked our natural rights," asked one anonymous reformer, "and thundered out his *anathemas* against the first advocate for them, in a manner, very ill-becoming him who occupies one of the first theological chairs in Europe?"[45]

When Rutherforth died in 1771, the subscription controversy was just entering its most intensive phase. For between July and September of that year, a group of reformers led by John Jebb met a number of times in Feather's Tavern to decide on appropriate measures for relief. After some dispute, they drafted a circular letter which called the Articles fallible doctrines "of dark and ignorant ages." Protesting loyalty to the established church, the document called only for the liberty of every man to judge for himself and not be compelled by law to subscribe. By January 1772, over two-hundred divines had signed the letter, including every member of Peterhouse and almost all of the Hyson Club.[46]

Yet, reform was an idea whose time had not come. In February 1772, a bill embodying the principles of the petition was presented to the House of Commons, where it was soundly defeated by a vote of 217 to 71. In a letter, Edward Gibbon congratulated his friend John Holroyd on

> the late victory of our dear mama the Church of England. She had last Thursday seventy-one rebellious sons, who pretended to set aside her will on account of insanity; but two-hundred-and-seventeen worthy champions, headed by Lord North, Burke, Hans Stanley, Charles Fox, Godfrey Clarke, etc., though they allowed the thirty-nine clauses of her testament were absurd and unreasonable, supported the validity of it with infinite humour.[47]

The reformers tried to localize their efforts, reasoning that if Parliament would not meet their grievances, perhaps the Cambridge Senate would be more understanding. But in the course of 1772, over ten attempts for relief again met defeat.[48]

Though Paley never signed the petition—in a regrettably flippant remark he said he "could not afford to keep a conscience"[49]—he did eventually demonstrate support for his liberal colleagues. Two years after Parliament had rejected the petition, a few Cambridge divines attempted to revive the issue. In a small pamphlet entitled "Considerations on the Propriety of Requiring a Subscription to Articles of Faith," Edmund Law essentially repeated Blackburne's arguments, maintaining there was no "tolerable excuse" for the existing practice. This drew a highly rhetorical reply from Thomas Randolph, Lady Margaret Professor of Divinity at Oxford, who reiterated the standard Tory objection to any church reform: if this change were made, the entire religious establishment would be weakened, then crumble.[50] The road to hell was paved with small reforms.

As his first published work, Paley chose to support Law by answering Randolph. "A Defence of the Considerations . . ." took Randolph to task, point by point, and gracefully reestablished the reformers' argument. The Thirty-nine Articles were deemed the product of "two or three men betwixt two and three centuries ago" who "fixed a multitude of obscure and dubious propositions which many millions after must bring themselves to believe."[51] Though Paley did not attach his name to the pamphlet, he had vindicated himself before his friends and demonstrated that he was firmly allied with the liberal reformers.

Paley's initial effort to dissociate himself from the furies of the subscription controversy, and his subsequent involvement in protecting the reputation of his mentor and patron Edmund Law, later drew stinging criticism for two, seemingly contradictory reasons. On the one hand, his jesting remark concerning the price of his conscience

—thereafter quoted frequently when Paley's name was mentioned—confirmed the worst fears of those who already believed the archdeacon to be a self-serving hypocrite devoid of a redeeming scruple. Thus, for example, Hazlitt spoke for a bevy of Romantics when he employed the remark as a representative summary of Paley's entire philosophy.[52] On the other hand, Paley's intimate social and intellectual ties with the Cambridge Latitudinarians persuaded a number of his later contemporaries that his ethics and politics bordered precariously on radicalism, a charge these detractors confirmed by pointing to certain passages in the *Principles*.[53] In either case, his reputation suffered unduly, especially considering that in the eighteenth century a few derogatory remarks in high places were sufficient to dash the ambitions of any aspiring divine.

The subscription controversy had another interesting effect on Paley's life and thought. One of the most trenchant defenders of the Articles had been Thomas Rutherforth, Regius Professor of Divinity and celebrated author of the *Institutes of Natural Law*, a required text in Paley's lecture course on moral philosophy. When Paley later refashioned his classroom notes into book form, he gratefully acknowledged in his preface each of his central sources, with the single exception of Rutherforth, his adversary of fifteen years before. If Paley never betrayed his friends, he never forgot his enemies either.[54]

When Paley departed Cambridge in May 1775 to accept the rectory of Musgrove, Cumberland, he expressed few regrets; he felt "he had enough of society, enough of amusement, and enough of study." As a student or tutor, he had resided in Cambridge for well over a decade, and perhaps he thought it was time to expand his horizons. Or perhaps the reason lay in a regulation that more than once cost the university a valuable teacher. Cambridge did not allow its fellows to marry; and within a few months of Paley's departure, he was engaged to Jane Hewitt, the daughter of a spirits merchant in Carlisle. In June, 1776, they were married.[55]

Paley's years as a fellow had registered a profound, perhaps even decisive influence on his mind. They provided him with the opportunity and leisure time to ponder the major ethical, political, and metaphysical tenets of the Enlightenment and, in his role as lecturer, to develop a method and style of composition he adhered to for the rest of his life. All Paley's works display a clarity, economy, and precision that characterize the best college textbooks; and it is probable that the shrewd archdeacon had his eye on just such a market when he composed them. More important, his years at the university had furnished him with a set of working assumptions and ideas that he expanded and qualified during his years in the North Country. With its political controversies and opportunities for intellectual companionship, Cambridge had fired his imagination to complete a system of philosophy that was already settling in his mind.

IV

Paley spent the remainder of his life as a clergyman, first in the pleasant rural communities of Appleby and Dalston from 1776 to 1782, then in Carlisle from 1782 to 1795, and finally in Durham and Lincoln from 1795 until his death in 1805. Like other eighteenth-century pluralists, he derived his income from a number of livings, even though, as in the case of Musgrove—a post he held for over twenty-five years—he never took up residence and preached only occasionally. Then, too, some of his positions were virtually sinecures, including his most exalted post in the ecclesiastical hierarchy, the archdeaconry of Carlisle. Although he never experienced the abject poverty that plagued many of the lesser clergy of his era, he attained genuine affluence only in 1795 when, as a reward for his *Evidences*, he was

translated to the lucrative rectorship of Bishop-Wearmouth, near Durham.[56] Most of his life he lived comfortably, but not conspicuously.

The daily routine of his existence varied little during
these years; he discharged his clerical duties conscien-
tiously and proficiently; he involved himself in the domestic chores of raising a family; he studied and reflected
upon the traditions of Enlightenment theology. With the
exception of his participation in the movement to abolish
the slave trade, he never enmeshed himself in partisan
politics, for which he expressed only the detached interest
of a philosopher. After his family, his central concern was
his writing, which he performed in solitude and with little
outside encouragement.

Following his departure from Cambridge in the early
summer of 1776, one of his first duties as rector of a small
North Country church was the regular composition of
sermons. This was not an entirely novel task for the young
divine, since as a lecturer on the Greek Testament at
Cambridge, he had taught the proper form and method of
delivering sermons. "As to preaching," he once counseled
his students, "if your situation requires a sermon every
Sunday, make one and steal five."[57] This advice notwithstanding, he himself borrowed only from his own material;
the manuscripts of his sermons reveal that he preached
some of his favorites over a dozen times, each, of course, to
a different congregation.[58]

These weekly productions, eventually selected and published in his complete works, reveal a more pessimis-
tic, emotional, and anxious theologian than emerges from
his more famous writings. "He who has not felt the weakness of his nature . . . has reflected little upon the subject of
religion"; "the first requisite of religion is seriousness."
"When we come . . . to confess our sins, let memory do its
office faithfully. Let these sins rise up before our eyes."[59]
Paley knew that religion came from within, that Chris-

tianity must, in Keats's phrase, be proven upon the pulses. As a preacher, his son tells us, he "carried all his powers and all his heart into the pulpit. . . . He seemed anxious to catch the spirit of devotion rather than be attentive to its form." In one of his more eloquent sermons, he characterized the meaning of Christian piety thus:

> When it is present, it gives life to every act of worship which we perform. . . . It is felt in our most retired moments, in our beds, our closets, our rides, our walks. It is stirred within us, when we are assembled with our children and servants in family prayer. It leads us to church . . . and it returns us to our homes holier, and happier, and better; and lastly, what greatly enhances its value to every anxious Christian, it affords to himself a proof that his heart is right towards God.[60]

Paley lamented what he called "a coldness in our devotions, which argues a decay of religion amongst us" and pleaded for "more and more insight into the deep and numerous corruptions of our heart, our lives and conversation." Such a struggle against religious indifference was an uphill battle, however, since "nothing is so hard to be accomplished as reformation; nothing so difficult as to change the heart."[61]

This preoccupation with man's alienation from God and the corollary that only through a profound inner transformation could a believer participate in Christ's redemption united Paley with the mainstream of Christian tradition. The piety manifest in his sermons revealed a theologian whose personal feelings and spiritual aspirations bore a closer resemblance to those of the Evangelical than to those of the deist. They portray a Christian who did not repudiate Original Sin or the indispensability of frequent and searching self-examinations—a Christian, in short, whose published theology was a rational confirmation of his beliefs rather than an accurate reflection of his faith.

This is not to say that his sermons contradict either the tone or spirit of his published theology, but, rather, that they augment those writings with precisely the elements of devotion and seriousness which nineteenth-century critics accused their Enlightenment predecessors of lacking. Paley's sermons reveal a dimension of his mind which the intellectual tradition of rational religion was either loath to admit or, more probably, assumed as axiomatic to the exercise. By its very method and goals, the rational justification of natural and revealed religion precluded individual statements of intense, emotional commitment.

After Paley became archdeacon of Carlisle in 1782, he entered the most productive phase of his career. In 1785, he published his *Principles of Moral and Political Philosophy,* an immediate success which was adopted for use in examinations at Cambridge within the year. Then in 1790, he published his most original but least popular study, *Horae Paulinae,* a labored exegesis of certain "undesigned coincidences" in the Acts and letters of Paul. Four years later, in 1794, he completed his analysis of revelation with the *Evidences of Christianity,* a masterpiece of Christian apologetics that garnered for him a flattering variety of honors and preferments, including a Doctorate of Divinity from Cambridge in 1795. In the space of nine years, he had catapulted himself from obscurity and become one of the most respected theologians in England.

Yet, despite the preferments that flowed in as a consequence of the *Evidences,* Paley never attained the bishopric that many thought he deserved. Various explanations were offered for this neglect, none of them definitive. His son thought that his father's failure to secure promotion was the result of his "almost too unlimited indulgence of wit and drollery," but most observers pointed to statements in the *Principles* which might have generated alarm

in a regime that was never praised for its ideological
flexibility. These included passages which seemed to
question the justness of the economic system and others
which maintained the right of revolution.[62] But there were
other, less political views in the book that perturbed his
readers. Thus, for example, Lord Granville was "a little
confounded at finding that some of his injunctions respecting keeping the Sabbath in the Fourth Command-
ment applied exclusively to the Jews." "This and the
chapter on toleration," he continued, "the King pointed
out to Mr. Pitt, saying 'Not orthodox, not orthodox' in
answer to Mr. Pitt's recommendation of him for a Bishop."
In this same vein, an anonymous writer in the *Gentleman's
Magazine* suggested that opposition "from a very high
quarter in the Church . . . rendered the recommendation
ineffectual," a thesis disputed, however, by Henry Gunning, who detected Wilberforce as the culprit.[63]

Paley himself never expressed either bitterness or regret
over his lack of promotion, probably because he was never
sufficiently ambitious to subject himself to the compro-
mises and petty humiliations which a successful career in
the church demanded. At Cambridge, he had never in-
dulged in "rooting," his own picturesque term for boosting
one's own career by abjectly courting the influential.
When he was composing the *Principles*, he brushed aside
the warning of John Law that he should remove the pigeon
analogy lest it cost him a bishopric, saying "Well, bishop
or no bishop, it shall stand." He turned down the mastership of Jesus in 1789 even though he was well aware the
post might have led to higher preferment. Thus, there
appears no reason to question Meadley's statement that
Paley always "appeared well-satisfied with the lot assigned him."[64]

When the French Revolution erupted in 1789, setting
off shock waves of discontent and fear throughout the
English countryside, Paley assumed a critical posture en-

tirely consistent with his *Principles* of four years before. True, in that book he had underscored Locke's right of revolution whenever a government abdicated its responsibilities, but the frantic accusations and impossible demands of Tom Paine were simply not what Paley had in mind. When he discovered a copy of the *Rights of Man* in his own household, he angrily threw it into the fireplace. In 1792 he published a reply to Paine, "Reasons for Contentment," which cautioned against "impious" complaints directed toward the government and the social system. "The laws which accidentally cast enormous estates into one great man's possession," he reminded his readers, "are, after all, the self-same laws which protect and guard the poor man." Moreover, the simple life of the poor was not without its "inestimable blessings;" it provided "a consistent train of employment both to body and mind;" it avoided the debauchery and licentiousness that often debilitate the rich; it offered the security and comfort of knowing one's station in life. To covet the fortunes of the rich or "to wish to seize them by force . . . [was] not only wickedness, but folly, as mistaken in the end as in the means."[65]

"Reasons for Contentment" provoked a number of bitter replies: "What reason could be given why we labourers ought to be contented, by a man who never worked in his life?" one asked pointedly.[66] Yet, if the archdeacon's tract occasionally displayed surprising depths of naiveté and even outright foolishness, its central argument came directly from the *Principles* and stemmed from the same impulse that probably led Paley to decline the mastership of Jesus. This was the belief that the elemental constituents of human happiness—health, friendship, self-control, work—were accessible to every human being and bore no relation to one's rank in society. "Our position is," he wrote in the *Principles*, "that happiness does not consist in greatness." Consequently, to change the government or disband the great estates accomplished little; it was, as he put it in "Reasons," "not only to venture out to sea in a storm, but to venture out for nothing."[67] In Paley's life and thought, there were elements of not only Epicureanism, but Stoicism as well.

Yet despite the fact that his reaction against the French Revolution was entirely consistent with his earlier, more tolerant political thinking, there can be no doubt that his works of the 1790s betrayed a stiffness, a hardening of the arteries, that manifested itself most forcibly in the legalistic tone of his later theology. *Horae Paulinae* attempted to refute "a supposition of forgery . . . as to the authenticity of the epistles" and *Evidences of Christianity*—the name itself embodies overtones of the law—purported "to offer a defence of Christianity which every Christian might read, without seeing the tenets in which he had been brought up attacked or decried."[68] The legalistic approach pervading both the method and literary style of his biblical criticism had its genesis in Paley's earlier days, when as a young man he often attended law courts both in Lancaster and at London's Old Bailey. As his son tells us, he was "particularly attached to that closeness . . . precision, keenness, and deep penetration, which are eminently called forth in the bar" and "used to think himself formed for a lawyer, both from his fondness for such sort of pointed investigation . . . and his cleverness in weighing evidence."[69]

Yet, if his legalism imbued his later works with an organizational efficiency and rhetorical power that were lacking in his earlier, more relaxed productions, it also imposed limitations on his analysis which sometimes impoverished his theology. As a brilliant advocate for the cause of Christianity, he occasionally stacked the deck in his own favor, emphasizing those facts which suited his purpose, impatiently dismissing those which did not. His considerable talents as a polemicist thus vitiated his objectivity, eliminating the willingness to experiment with ideas which characterized the best portions of the *Principles*.

From 1795 until his death in 1805, Paley divided his residence between Lincoln, where he spent his summer months, and Bishop-Wearmouth, where his magnificent house, "one of the best parsonages in all England," was surrounded by a lovely park which enjoyed a commanding view of the Wear. In 1796 he remarried—his first wife had died in 1791, having borne him eight children—and settled once again into the peaceful domestic routine that had characterized his life since he left Cambridge. His son provides a portrait of him during these final years, taking a morning stroll with his youngest daughter.

> At such times he seldom spoke a single word; but now and then he used to surprise his little companion by bursting out into the most immoderate laughter, or mouthing out scraps of poetry, or sentences of prose—quite enough to show that these were seasonable exercises both for his mind and body. With the handle of his stick in his mouth, now moving in a short hurried step, now stopping at a butterfly, a flower, a snail; at one instant pausing to consider the subject of his next sermon, at the next carrying the whole weight and intent of his mind to the arranging some pots in his greenhouse . . . he presented the most prominent feature of his mind very obviously, but made it perhaps happy for his public character that he chose to be alone.[70]

Now known throughout the country, the archdeacon received visits from the philosopher James Mackintosh and the classicist Richard Porson.[71] He had new responsibilities; for a short time he served as a justice of the peace, bringing upon himself a wave of unpopularity by attempting to limit the licenses for new public houses. But he poured most of his energy into a new book, his *mag-*

num opus, the study that would complete his philosophic system.

He knew he was running out of time. In 1800, he began to suffer severe stomach complaints that forced him to abandon most of his formal clerical duties. Yet this enforced "leisure was not lost." "It was only in my study," he wrote, "that I could repair my deficiencies in the church: it was only through the press that I could speak."[72] In 1802, he saw the publication of his *Natural Theology,* his final work, which, like the *Evidences* of eight years before, attracted wide attention and applause throughout Britain. The name of Paley, said the *Edinburgh Review,* "was probably associated with as large and as enviable a portion of public approbation as that of any living ecclesiastic."[73] On May 25, 1805, at the peak of his fame, he finally succumbed to the illness that had crippled him during the last years of his life. He was buried in Carlisle cathedral.

CHAPTER 2

The Triumph of Hume
and the Problem of Paley

NEAR THE END OF DAVID HUME's *Dialogues concerning Natural Religion*, Philo, whose "careless scepticism" has challenged, bewildered, and consistently frustrated the elegant reasoning of Cleanthes, rashly asserts that all religious systems suffer from "great and insuperable difficulties." "Each disputant triumphs in his turn; while he carries on an offensive war, and exposes the absurdities, barbarities, and pernicious tenets of his antagonist. But all of them, on the whole, prepare a complete triumph for the *Sceptic*."[1] To every argument proposed by his skilled and often persuasive antagonists, Philo unveils equally compelling counter arguments whose cumulative effect, according to most modern observers, justifies Philo's somewhat premature claim to victory. Norman Kemp Smith the distinguished editor of the best edition of the *Dialogues*, considers Philo's arguments "final and complete"; Peter Gay argues that "little, very little, remains of the 'religious hypothesis' after this assault"; and Sir Leslie Stephen, whose two-volume study of the English Enlightenment still dominates the field after a century of vigorous scholarship, calls Hume's skepticism "one of the great turning-points in the history of thought."[2]

Yet, for well over a century after Hume launched his urbane vendetta against the metaphysics of his venerated predecessors, the argument from design flourished in orthodox circles and even, it might be claimed, experienced a renascence. At the center of this revival was William Paley, whose *Natural Theology*, published in 1802, repeated virtually every one of Cleanthes' arguments, while at the same time adding an enormous amount of fresh empirical verification. In essence, Paley utterly ignored Hume's objections, and the tremendous popularity of his work offers further testimony to the commonplace but often forgotten assertion that Hume was an isolated figure in his own time. As Hume himself tells us in his brief, remarkable autobiography, the *Treatise of Human Nature* "*fell dead-born from the press*, without reaching such distinction, as even to excite a murmur among the zealots,"[3] and when critical reaction to his philosophy eventually did appear, it was short and unfailingly hostile. William Warburton, the influential Bishop of Gloucester, denounced him as "an atheistical Jacobite, a monster as rare with us as a hippogriff"; Samuel Johnson once left the room when he saw Hume entering; and, finally, it is always sobering to note that Hume wished his *Dialogues* published posthumously because, as he put it in a letter, he was "desirous to live quietly, and keep remote from all Clamour."[4] Though Hume would wake Immanuel Kant from his "dogmatic slumber," in Britain he was a solitary figure, a philosopher with few genuine admirers.

This isolation poses an interesting problem for the historian of ideas; for if Hume's arguments were "final and complete," why were they so systematically ignored? What threat did they pose to the men who read them? Why were the tenets of natural religion so slow to die? In attempting to understand the mind of William Paley, we must begin by probing the isolation of David Hume, whose critical philosophy, our most penetrating critics tell us, demolished the arguments of the archdeacon twenty years prior to their formulation.

As we shall see, the reason Hume's "triumph" was not apparent to late eighteenth- and early nineteenth-century readers centers on two interrelated points. First, natural theology was the spiritual core of the British Enlightenment. In its methodology and assumptions, it was completely compatible with the "new science," providing eager scientists with a convincing metaphysical justification for their research. It was a citadel around which scientists, theologians, moralists, and political thinkers could rally, despite individual differences on matters of detail, and it functioned as the center of an intellectual consensus so pervasive, that it remained healthy and vigorous deep into the nineteenth century. When Hume attacked the foundations of natural religion, he shattered —at least theoretically—that fundamental unity, and with nothing positive to substitute in its place, his skepticism was easily defeated by the scathing ridicule of the Common Sense school and the soothing reassertions of William Paley.

Second, Hume gravely underestimated the emotional underpinnings of natural theology. Though his philosophy asserted the efficacy of belief and custom both in epistemology and in religion, his was not the fideistic skepticism of a Pascal or a Demea. Hume assumed, as did John Wesley and William Wilberforce, that the arid rationalism of natural religion was the sole foundation of orthodox Christianity in the eighteenth century. By challenging it on its own terms and with its own logic, he thought he could drive this scourge from the human mind and build philosophy upon a firmer, more scientific foundation.[5]

It is one of the theses of this chapter, and of this work in general, that natural religion was, however, only the visible intellectual expression of a deeply held Christian faith which eschewed emotionalism because of the untoward excesses of the religious enthusiasts. Few natural theologians—certainly not William Paley—believed that their elaborate proofs would actually convince the nonbeliever or the atheist. Natural theologians wrote for each other; they cast their Christianity into forms which generations of reasonable men had found most palatable. It is our own bias, stemming perhaps from the Romantics, which suggests that somehow the orthodox Demea is more "religious" than the rationalist Cleanthes; that to be authentically Christian one must undergo the emotional transformations experienced by Victorian Evangelicals. In his Christianity, Paley was as sincere—and as intractable—as Evangelicals such as Charles Simeon or Isaac Milner.

II

To understand Hume's failure to dismantle natural religion, it is first necessary to examine the procedures and aspirations of the "new science." The conflict between religious faith and practical science, felt so keenly by the Victorians, rarely disturbed Enlightenment scientists because they based their faith on an argument which in its assumptions and methods corresponded to those of the laboratory. This argument was articulated by many scientists, but the "Rules of Reasoning" embodied in Newton's *Principia* offers a useful summary and, more important, a clue to understanding the complex relationship between Enlightenment science and theology.

Though in practice Newton's scientific method involved a complex interplay of inductive and deductive thinking, he stressed the primacy of induction in the *Principia*. Of his four "Rules," both numbers three and four explicitly revealed this love of empirical procedure: "In experimental philosophy," he wrote in Rule Four, "we are to look upon propositions inferred by general induction as accurately or very nearly true . . . till such time as other phenomena occur, by which they may either be made more accurate, or liable to exception."[6] Less than a hundred years before, Bacon had become the prophet of the "new science" by his insistence on the inductive

method, and if he was something of an unfaithful servant
to his own philosophy—he rejected the advanced theories
of Harvey, Gilbert, Copernicus, and Kepler[7]—his appeal
struck deep into the minds of seventeenth-century scientists. "For now the Genius of Experimenting is so much
dispenc'd," Thomas Sprat proudly recorded in his *History
of the Royal Society,* "that even in this *Nation,* if there
were one, or two such Assemblies settled; there could not
be wanting able men enough to carry them on."[8]

Now the argument from design, which dominated natural theology, was inductive in method. Unlike the on-
tological argument, it depended on the direct observation
of natural processes for its assertion that God existed.
Bacon was getting at the a posteriori character of the
argument when he defined natural theology as "that
knowledge . . . concerning God which may be obtained by
the contemplation of his creatures; which knowledge may
be truly divine in respect of the object, and natural in
respect of the light."[9] In natural religion, God lived in the
detail.

Yet in its emphasis on final causes, the teleological argument shared more with Peripatetic science than with
the experimental philosophy of the seventeenth century.
Teleological reasoning obstructed meaningful progress in
science because it always involved a form of tautology;
instead of asking how something comes about—how, for
example, the eye sees—it sought to answer the more metaphysical question of why; thus the eye saw because it was
the function of the eye to see. In his *Dialogue on the Great
World Systems,* Galileo pleaded against the use of telic
explanations and urged the pragmatic separation of science and religion. Similarly, Bacon censured the intru-
sion of teleology into science because "the handling of final
causes . . . hath intercepted the severe and diligent inquiry
of all real and physical causes."[10] In coming to terms with
the scientific revolution, one might assume that most

thinkers gratefully accepted the advice of Galileo and Bacon.

It is often astonishing, therefore, to find how seventeenth-century scientists actually argued. For in their writings the concept of final cause not only was present, it occasionally seems to have directly affected how they investigated their material. Knowing there was evidence of design in one process of nature, they would seek it in another, yet unexplored process. Consider the case of William Harvey, whose discoveries concerning the circulation of the blood mark a major achievement of the new science. In a reminiscence, Robert Boyle remarked that Harvey's awareness of design in nature, of the adaption of means to ends, inspired his most famous discovery.

> And I remember, that when I asked our famous *Harvey*, in the only Discourse I had with him, . . . What were the things that had induc'd him to think of a *Circulation of the Blood?* He answer'd me, that when he took notice that the Valves in the Veins of so many several parts of the Body, were so plac'd that they gave free passage to the Blood Towards the Heart, but oppos'd the passage of the Veinal Blood the Contrary way: He was invited to imagine, that so Provident a Cause as Nature had not so Plac'd so many Valves without Design: and no Design seem'd more possible than that, since the Blood could not well, because of the interposing Valves, be Sent by the Veins to the Limbs; it should be Sent through the Arteries, and Return through the Veins, whose Valves did not oppose its course that way.[11]

In Harvey's case, an inclusion of final cause proved no restriction to genuine scientific discovery; even though he seemed to proceed from the fact of design in nature and then work out the details—the reverse of what might be expected—his investigation involved something more than the circular logic of the Peripatetics.

Less satisfactory results for the development of science occurred in biology, where the meshing of inductive Ba-

conian science and the argument from design was typified
by the influential naturalist John Ray. His *Wisdom of God
Manifested in the Works of Creation* was published in
1691, and by 1735 had raced through ten editions. Unlike
his ardent disciple, William Derham, Ray was no amateur
scientist; he was a member of the Royal Society whose
work in botany and zoology earned him the reputation as
the most distinguished naturalist of his day. Yet, for all his
credentials, the scientific discussions in his most popular
work bore a closer resemblance to Aristotle than would
seem appropriate for a proper Baconian.

> If we consider the manner of the Rain's descent, distilling
> down gradually and by drops, which is most convenient for
> the watering of the Earth; whereas if it should fall down in a
> continual Stream, like a River, it would gall the Ground,
> wash away Plants by the Roots, overthrow Houses, and
> greatly incommode, if not suffocate Animals; If, I say, we
> consider these things and many more that might be added,
> we might in this respect also cry out with the Apostle, *O the
> depths of the Riches both of the Wisdom and Knowledge of
> God!*

Or, on the subject of the *"erect Posture* of the Body of
Man"*:

> It is more commodious for the sustaining of the Head, which
> being full of Brains and very heavy (the Brain in Man being
> far larger in proportion to the Bulk of his Body than in any
> other animal) would have been very painful and wearisome
> to carry, if the Neck had lain parallel or inclining to the
> Horizon.[12]

Countless other examples could be reproduced from the
scientific literature of the era, but for our purposes, Ray
shall speak for them all. His excursions into natural
science convincingly illustrate how teleological reasoning
bound inseparably together the science and theology of

the Enlightenment. Natural theologians used the findings of science to herald their claim that God, in Ray's words, "celebrates his Wisdom in the Creation" and scientists, conversely, used the argument from design to buttress their own faith and prove to all challengers that the exploration of nature led men out of the wilderness of atheism into the fold of religion.[13]

Yet, there was a danger. The doctrine of final causes might be good religion but, as science, it was unacceptable, and here was a Scylla and Charybdis that not everyone successfully navigated. If teleological explanations were used exclusively, as with the naturalists, there was the pitfall outlined by Bacon and Galileo; final causes explained nothing. If, on the other hand, they were divorced from scientific investigations, as in Descartes, the scientist would prove only that the universe had order, not purpose. Historians of science agree that Newton successfully charted his way through these troubled waters, that neither religious metaphors nor finalist theology obstructed his mathematical physics. Only after completing his analysis did he recognize God as the efficient cause of the universe, though he stipulated that the deity might occasionally intervene to keep the mechanism in working order.[14]

Newton himself, however, was far less certain about the distinct separation of science and theology in the *Principia*. In a letter to Richard Bentley, he remarked that he had written his treatise with "an Eye upon such Principles as might work with considering Men for the belief of a Deity; and nothing can rejoice me more than to find it useful for that Purpose."[15] Then too, in an *Account of Sir Isaac Newton's Philosophical Discourses*—the most accurate and readable of the popularizations—Colin Maclaurin spoke of "how essential the greatest and best philosophers have thought the consideration of final causes to be to true philosophy, without which it wants the greatest beauty, perfection, and use. It gave particular pleasure to Sir Isaac Newton to see that his philosophy had contributed to promote an attention to them . . . after *Descartes* and others endeavored to banish them."[16] Newton obviously misperceived the implications of his own world system, and his confusion over the role of teleology in science foreshadowed an even larger confusion in the Enlightenment. To scientists of the Royal Society such as Boyle, an insistence on induction did not preclude telic explanations since it was the argument from design which provided their investigations with meaning and purpose.

Newton's two pronouncements on induction comprised his third and fourth "Rules of Reasoning in Philosophy." We have dealt with them initially because the experimental method was considered the triumph of seventeenth-century science. Yet it was his second rule which lay at the heart of his work; "to the same natural effects, we must, as far as possible, assign the same causes."[17] The significance of this assumption for modern science need not be elaborated; without uniformity in nature, inferences from induction, and consequently any meaningful generalization, would be impossible.

Absolutely critical for science, this same assumption buttressed the thinking of natural theologians and explained one of their most frequent arguments, the appeal to consensus. "Now for *Adoration* or *Religious Worship*," wrote Henry More in his *Antidote against Atheism*, "it is as universal as mankind, there being no Nation under the Cope of heaven that does not do divine worship to something or other, . . . wherefore according to the ordinary *naturall light* that is in all men, there is a God."[18] In a similar vein, Ralph Cudworth devoted most of his *True Intellectual System of the Universe* to proving "that the most intelligent of the ancient Pagans, notwithstanding the multiplicity of gods worshipped by them, did generally acknowledge one supreme [and] omnipotent Deity."[19]

One manifestation of this appeal to the *"universal Observation* of men in all times and places"—as Sprat put it—was the admiration heaped on Galen. His persistent invocation of the design argument, especially in *De usa partium,* persuaded men like Ray and Derham that the idea of God transcended the boundaries of time and space. "There appears to me as much Divinity in Galen," Thomas Browne observed, "as in Suarez' *Metaphysics."*[20]

The assumption of causal uniformity at the core of both the new science and natural religion was also a critical factor in the deist controversy of the early eighteenth century. In a sense, the deists were no more than consistent natural theologians who, with rigor and courage, applied the maxim that "like effects proceed from like causes," Newton's second rule of reasoning. "How can it be conceived," Matthew Tindal asked in his *Christianity as Old as the Creation,* "that God's Laws, whether internally or externally reveal'd, are not at all times the same, when the Author of them is, and has been, universally the same for ever?"[21] For the deists, the question thus became why revelation, unlike natural religion, was restricted only to certain peoples and, if so, why an omnipotent, omnipresent, and beneficent Creator would limit the only path to salvation to a relatively primitive people in the eastern Mediterranean.[22]

Yet, despite the bitter debates following each publication of this new heresy, deist and orthodox shared common ground. "We are to admit no more causes of natural things than such as are both true and sufficient to explain their appearances"—this was Newton's first "Rule of Reasoning," which, like his second injunction, provided the conceptual framework for both practical science and natural religion, both deist and orthodox, in the Enlightenment.[23] In the early seventeenth century, Lord Herbert of Cherbury had reduced religion to six common notions; later, Locke asked of Christians only a belief in the Mes-

siah;[24] throughout the Enlightenment, most natural theologians could distill their creed into three propositions: God exists; he should be worshiped; there is eternal
life. The difference between deist and orthodox turned less
on a philosophical distinction than a psychological fear.
What the deists wanted to simplify and make consistent—the Revelation of the Lord—the orthodox fought
with blind fury to maintain. At a critical point, the issue
became not simply belief, but faith itself.

Nevertheless, the actual intellectual disagreement sep-
arating religious adversaries was limited; deists, orthodox
Christians, scientists, and theologians shared the same
assumptions, the same aspirations. The significance of natural theology within this broad consensus, especially in
the relationship between science and religion, cannot be
underestimated. It was not simply an adjunct to science,
not simply the fee scientists paid for examining their
Father's house, but the very goal of scientific experiment,
its metaphysical rationale. "We are to endeavor to rise,
from the effects through immediate causes, to the Supreme Cause," Maclaurin wrote in his popularization of
Newton: "We are from his works, to seek to know God
and . . . thus natural philosophy may become a sure basis
for natural religion."[25] The proliferation of teleological
reasoning, long after Bacon warned against it, demonstrated that neither scientist nor theologian could dwell
comfortably in a world explicated only by efficient causes,
a world devoid of meaning save for charts and equations.
The argument from design gave meaning to science, and
science offered powerful ammunition for the argument
from design.

This relationship was unique to England and arguably
one of the defining characteristics of the Enlightenment in
Britain. In Germany, the *Aufklärung* followed the power-
fully synthetic, though often ambiguous rationalism of
Gottfried Wilhelm Leibniz, whose disputes with both

Newton and Locke steered German philosophy down a unique line of inquiry culminating in an intellectual revolution of major proportions one century later. Leibniz's attack on Newton, embodied in the *Leibniz-Clarke Correspondence,* concerned the notions of Absolute Space and Time which Newton had employed in drawing up his calculations. Like many Continental critics, Leibniz thought gravity was but another unexplained "occult quality" and he considered Newton's belief that space was a "sensorium of God" as a metaphysical atrocity. These objections were answered patiently and with great intelligence by Samuel Clarke, the famed English rationalist whose scientific works and Boyle lectures established him as a worthy spokesman for the shy Newton.[26]

Yet, even after five letters and five replies, there was no real agreement on any substantial issue. Leibniz's mind, like the philosophic system he created, was a closed affair with the Principle of Sufficient Reason and the Principle of the Identity of Indiscernibles as its lock and key.[27] It was not that the overall purpose of Leibniz's philosophy was radically different from that of the English natural scientists and theologians. Both wanted to find some accommodation between mechanism and teleology, between a world of things and a universe of God. But Leibniz was an ontologist and Newton an empiricist; and between the *Monadology* and the *Opticks* yawned a gap in methods and in assumptions that was not easily bridged.

This difference was again thrown into sharp relief when in his *New Essays concerning Human Understanding* Leibniz sharply criticized Lockean epistemology. Deeming it shallow and facile, Leibniz substituted his own concept of the monad, which for human psychology meant that knowledge was not the combined product of sensation and reflection, as with Locke, but was entirely contained within the individual monads and gradually unfolded or made conscious by the stimulus of external sensation. Since each monad reflected in its own unique manner the whole universe, knowledge became an internal and necessarily incomplete evolution of that which was always present in the mind.[28] Unlike Locke, Leibniz provided an epistemology which was dynamic, telic, and utterly consistent with his metaphysics and theology. His critique of Locke thus became something more than a quibble over the existence of innate ideas; it was the clash of two philosophies that at bottom shared little of fundamental importance.[29]

It was Leibniz, not Locke or Newton, who dominated German thought in the eighteenth century. Under the aegis of Christian Wolff, a modified and in some ways painfully distorted philosophy of Leibniz would be frozen into a score of textbooks that for two generations influenced young German minds. Leibniz was not without his critics: Pierre Louis Moreau de Maupertuis and Leonhard Euler, both influential scientists and mathematicians, clung to Newtonian empiricism and even attempted to reconcile it with the dogmatic injunctions of Wolff and his disciples. But it would take the synthesis of Kant late in the century to draw together British empiricism and German rationalism.[30]

In France, the dominance of the Catholic church on all facets of society forced intellectuals to choose sides and engage in nothing less than an intellectual civil war. Here there was no possibility of a consensus between skeptic and orthodox, between scientist and theologian. Though "enlightened" individuals existed on both sides, as R. R. Palmer has shown,[31] the philosophes spent their lives trying to obtain for France what had existed in England since the end of the seventeenth century. This struggle for intellectual freedom, religious tolerance and some form of representative government ultimately bore fruit in the upheavals of 1789, but for most of the century it meant that the philosophes could devote less time than the British to, say, the metaphysical complexities of space and time, and engaged instead in various and often brilliantly subtle forms of political polemic.[32]

Moreover, as Aram Vartanian has demonstrated, it was the influence of the Cartesians rather than of Newton that formed the mainstream of the French Enlightenment; and the Cartesian world-view was inimical to teleological reasoning. In England, Descartes had been attacked by both Cudworth and Ray for, as Ray put it, "banishing all consideration of final Causes," but in France their warnings fell on deaf ears. Certainly there were French thinkers who advocated the argument from design; the Abbé Pluché's *Histoire du ciel* provided hundreds of examples of Newtonian finalist theology; and Voltaire, though critical of the absurdities of teleological reasoning, defended its proper use in his *Philosophical Dictionary*.[33] But far more representative of French scientific thinking were the philosophers and naturalists who, inspired by Cartesian mechanistic biology, repudiated teleological reasoning and reduced the order of nature to matter and motion. Denis Diderot; Julien Offray de La Mettrie; Georges Louis Leclerc, comte de Buffon; and their followers separated their science from any metaphysical considerations and transformed the dualism of their seventeenth-century mentor into the materialistic monism typical of the moral determinists.[34] Thus, for France it was the vortices of Descartes and not the empiricism of Bacon or Newton which liberated natural philosophy from the teleological reasoning of Peripatetic science. In its alliance of natural religion and empirical science, England stood alone.

III

Hume challenged this alliance by exposing the intrinsic uncertainties of its central assumptions; and in our own century, when the teleological argument no longer prompts men of good faith to behold the glory of God in the anatomical complexities of, say, the wing of a sea gull, his analysis seems cogent and undeniably prophetic. To every argument of the teleologists, Hume framed a logically compelling reply: he repudiated the method of natural theology by showing its reasoning to be rooted in the vicissitudes and arbitrary selectiveness of human experiences; he controverted the assumption behind the argument by drilling holes into the uniformitarian premise. He knew the power of rhetorical arguments and employed them shamelessly when it suited his purposes. He anticipated objections and encompassed them into his own analysis, often turning them to his own advantage. Though Hume wore the mantle of a philosopher, he was at bottom a psychologist whose central purpose was to understand why men believe as they do, and from that knowledge establish the parameters of truth.

He began by examining the assumption of causal uniformity. "*Like effects prove like causes,*" Philo remarks to Cleanthes in the *Dialogues;* "this is the experimental argument."[35] It was Hume's major contribution to the history of philosophy to prove this assumption incapable of logical demonstration. Yet, he never denied that cause-effect relationships might exist; "I never asserted so absurd a Proposition as *that any thing might arise without a Cause,*" he wrote a friend in 1754, "I only maintained, that our Certainty of the Falsehood of that Proposition proceeded neither from Intuition or Demonstration; but from another Source." That "Source" was custom or habit, "the great guide of human life."[36] Men believed in causal relationships because they had experienced them in the past; their predictive value, however, was severely limited. "There can be no demonstrative arguments to prove," Hume wrote in the *Treatise,* "that those instances of which we have had no experience, resemble those, of which we have had experience." Our knowledge that the sun will rise tomorrow rests strictly on "belief," which he defined as "a more vivid, lively, forcible, firm, steady conception of an object, than what the imagination alone is ever able to attain." What Hutchinson said of morals, Hume applied to epistemology; experience and instinct, not reason and logic, determined our knowledge of the outside world.[37]

When Hume applied this principle to natural religion, the results startled Cleanthes and all the theologians he represented. "We have no idea of the Supreme Being but what we learn from reflection on our own faculties," Hume wrote in the *Enquiry*,[38] and he encompassed in this claim two major arguments against the teleologists. First, he argued that there was no a priori justification for the supposed logical deduction that order was always the product of an orderer. "If we see a house," Philo tells Cleanthes, "we conclude, with greatest certainty, that it had an architect or builder, because this is precisely that species of effect, which we had experienced to proceed from that species of cause."[39] Order, design, final cause —these notions are principles of the mind, not matter; like the concept of beauty, they are formed in the eyes of the beholder and are not intrinsic to nature itself. This argument, which anticipated Kant and would be used by Mill a century later, radically undercut the major premise of the teleological proof; it traced the argument from design to a cognitive operation which may or may not bear a satisfactory relationship to what it described.

Moreover, the same psychological process which perceived order and design in nature, when applied to the enormous and uncertain task of describing the Deity, terminated in a repugnant anthropomorphism. Nothing amused Hume more than "our Inclination to find our own Figures in the Clouds, our Faces in the Moon, our Passions and Sentiments even in inanimate Matter." Such an inclination, he continued, "ought to be controlled, and can never be a legitimate Ground of Assent."[40] Yet if it amused him that men made themselves "the model of the Universe," it also appalled him. It appalled him that the highest religious feelings originated in the lowest human apprehensions; that religions began in fear and ended in hate; that men degraded the concept of God by projecting on him their basest emotions and their enduring anxieties.

> It is an absurdity to believe that the Deity has human passions, and one of the lowest of human passions, a restless appetite for applause. It is an inconsistency to believe, that, since the Deity has this human passion, he has not others also; and, in particular, a disregard to the opinions of creatures, so much inferior.[41]

Frightened men get the God they deserve; and, for Hume, the innumerable visions of the Deity conjured up by primitive societies in the past, coupled with the more rationalistic but no more consistent portrayals in his own age, only proved the unreliability of *any* conjecture about the nature of God.

It was this theme that Hume developed in his *Natural History of Religion*, where he assumed the same posture toward Christianity which Gibbon would so successfully exploit in *Decline and Fall of the Roman Empire*. Religions were not divinely inspired; they began, grew, flourished, and declined within specific historical contexts which accounted for their success or failure. For Gibbon, Christianity was both a product of and a reason for the decline of Rome; the *pietas* of the district governor was not the piety of the Christian martyr; no tough soldier lived by the injunctions of the Beatitudes. Hume, on the other hand, was less interested in one religion than in religions generally. His *History* was less history than anthropology. He posited the striking notion that initially men were polytheistic and only gradually became theists of the Christian variety. Among primitive peoples, "the first ideas of religion arise not from a contemplation of the works of nature, but from a concern with regard to the events of life, and from the incessant hopes and fears, which actuate the human mind." Later, "by a certain train of thinking," this anthropomorphism becomes refined until men restrict themselves to a single Deity, wise, omnipresent, and powerful. Yet, even though men worship only one Supreme Being, "they are guided to that notion, not by reason, of which they are in great measure incapable, but by the adulation and fears of the most vulgar superstition."[42] As before, Hume located the religious impulse not in reason, but in feeling, custom, and belief, in those sections of the mind where Cleanthes felt least comfortable and secure.

Hume's appeal to experience achieved its dramatic climax, however, when he discussed the one fact which natural theologians chose to ignore. Like Samuel Johnson, he believed in the existence of evil. "The first entrance into life gives anguish to the new-born infant and to his wretched parent," Philo laments in Book X; "weakness, impotence, distress, attend each stage of life: And it is at last finished in agony and horror." With existential weariness, Philo explores the landscape of human debasement; men are their own greatest enemy; they are condemned to eternal labor, haunted by fearful dreams, threatened by withering disease, ultimately "terrified, not bribed to the continuance of their existence." No longer indulgent to the sensibilities of his opponents, Philo finally springs the awkward questions which Epicurus asked of God: "Is he willing to prevent evil, but not able? then he is impotent. Is he able, but not willing? then is he malevolent. Is he both able and willing? whence then is evil?" The orthodox reply to these clever questions centers on the Fall of Man and it is to this refuge that Demea quickly retreats. But

Cleanthes, in an uncommon flash of intuition, suddenly realizes the thrust of Philo's attack; "Your long agreement with Demea did indeed a little surprise me; but I find you were all the while erecting a concealed battery against me."[43]

Hume's arguments stripped the natural theologians of the easy complacency which logically flowed from the teleological approach. In opposition to his orthodox antagonists, Hume denied that the Deity created a world which performed with the precision, efficiency, and predictability of the Strasbourg clock; rather, God forged a universe where the inhumanity and evil of his most favored creature, man himself, reflected the chaotic and enormously destructive powers of nature around him. This meant that either God was a malevolent and bungling fellow—laughable, save for his power—or that the assumption behind the argument from design erred at some critical juncture. Consistent with his usual humility and skepticism concerning metaphysics, Hume chose the latter alternative. He always knew what the Lisbon earthquake prompted Voltaire to discover: that the teleological argument encompassed only some of the facts, not all of them. It ignored the storms, earthquakes, plagues, and droughts which devastated the earth and made a mockery of optimism. Evil, like cancer, was an integral part of men and yet their enemy.[44]

The core of Hume's attack on natural theology and the central principle of his philosophy was that as a tool for unlocking the mysteries of man and the universe, reason was a limited and deceptively fallible guide. It could not answer the questions which, by its nature, it could not ignore. The major problems of metaphysics and epistemology were unquestionably rewarding to contemplate; only once in his works did Hume repudiate the endeavors of philosophy. But since these same questions were incapable of resolution, Hume condemned the intellectual arrogance and dogmatism of the great system-builders. His entire philosophy was a plea for humility.

> Let us become thoroughly sensible of the weakness, blindness, and narrow limits of human reason: Let us duly consider its uncertainty and needless contrarieties, even in subjects of common life and practice: Let the errors and deceits of our very senses by set before us; the insuperable difficulties, which attend first principles in all systems; the contradictions, which adhere to the very ideas of matter, cause and effect, extension, space, time, motion; and, in a word, quantity of all kinds, the object of the only science, that can fairly pretend to any certainty or evidence. When these topics are displayed in their full light, as they are by some philosophers and almost all divines; who can retain such confidence in this frail faculty of reason as to pay any regard to its determinations in points so sublime, so abstruse, so remote from common life and experience?[45]

In his own philosophy, Hume constantly employed the assumption of causal uniformity; it underlay his historical writings, his refutation of miracle stories, and his moral speculations. His only point was that, like many other assumptions, it could not be declared a certain truth.

Yet, there persisted throughout his philosophy a confusion which was largely responsible for his misinterpretation by the Common Sense school. It was never clear whether Hume believed that experience was simply a method of knowing the outside world or whether it constituted all knowledge and bore an unknown relationship to the real world. If he maintained the former, "objectivist" position, then cause-effect reasoning was imperfect, but ultimately reliable. If he assumed the latter, "subjectivist" stance, then men became tightly restricted in what they might know, and human reason became something of a trick the mind played on itself. Most modern scholars tend to interpret Hume as an "objectivist" and thereby blunt the cutting edge of his skepticism; they find in Hume the first solid statement of the modern theory of science.[46]

The Common Sense school, on the other hand, burdened Hume with the "subjectivist" position; and this interpretation had enormous implications for both science and theology.[47] In his *Inquiry into the Human Mind on the Principles of Common Sense,* published in 1764, Thomas Reid thought Hume had "built a system of scepticism, which leaves no ground to believe any one thing rather than its contrary." In Reid's view, Hume, like many of his famous predecessors including Berkeley and Locke, worked under the mistaken hypothesis "that nothing is perceived but which is in the mind which perceives it; that we do not really perceive things which are external, but only certain images and pictures of them, imprinted upon the mind, which are called *impressions* and *ideas.*" Worse, Berkeley abolished that external world and Hume refuted the "necessary connections" on which the mind depends for coherence and stability. For Reid, this was skepticism.[48]

Other members of the Common Sense school, notably James Oswald and James Beattie, borrowed their main ideas from Reid and, with regrettably less philosophic acumen, openly ridiculed Hume's major arguments. Thus Beattie, whose *Essay on the Nature and Immutability of Truth* far exceeded in popularity the works of Reid, could accuse Hume of "mistaking verbal analogies for real ones" and "giving plausibility to nonsense." The *Dialogues* he dismissed with a single sentence: "If the universe had a beginning, it must have had a cause." But he saved his most intense denunciations for the end of his book.

It is most certain, that he, if he is indeed the author of those Essays, and of that Treatise, hath exerted his great talents . . . in endeavoring to persuade the world, that the fundamental doctrines of natural religion are irrational, and the proofs of revealed religion such as ought not satisfy an impartial mind; and that there is not in any science an evidence of truth sufficient to produce certainty. . . . When a sceptic attacks one principle of common sense, he does in effect attack all; for if we are made distrustful of the veracity of instinctive conviction in one instance, we must . . . become distrustfull in every other. A little scepticism introduced into science will soon assimilate the whole to its own nature; the fatal fermentation, once begun, spreads wider and wider evey [sic] moment, till all the mass be transformed into rottenness and poison.[49]

To Reid, Beattie, Oswald, and most of their contemporaries, Hume was a thoroughgoing and uncompromising skeptic; and since it was the peculiar strength of natural religion that it drew its arguments from the same assumptions and the same proofs as natural science, by attacking one, Hume also discredited the other. In attempting to expose the shabby thinking behind most metaphysics, Hume had annihilated the basis of natural science as well. His dispute with uniformitarianism may have demonstrated the impossibility of proving God's existence, but it had also cast doubt on the precise calculations of Newton. If Hume had simply maintained that our knowledge of God was drastically limited, it might have been acceptable. Had not the devout theologian William Law said the same thing? But in attacking the principles and assumptions of natural religion, Hume proved science to be equally unreliable. And this violated common sense. Those who had refuted Berkeley by kicking a stone or inviting him to walk off a cliff could disprove Hume with the same simple expedients. "A Philosopher," wrote Oswald, "cannot with safety to his own character, set himself above the common sense of mankind."[50]

Moreover, by making teleological reasoning a product of mind alone, Hume banished final causes from the reality of the world; he made them internal fabrications rather than eternal truths testifying to God's power and wisdom. The danger was obvious. Without final causes, the universe and everything within it existed without purpose and without meaning. This had been Newton's fear and the major reason he refused to eliminate final causes from both the *Principia* and the *Opticks,* even though, technically, his formula and calculations could be separated from his metaphysics. It had been the reason Boyle insisted on the subservience of natural science to theology and the guiding principle behind the famous lecture series that bore his name. It had been responsible for the survival of Peripatetic categories in biology and the curious, often fantastic explanations of the earth's age and origin. In short, it had been the raison d'être of science in the British Enlightenment.

To the Common Sense school, Hume's repudiation of teleology thus became an extraordinary act of pure destruction. Acceptance of his ideas would "subvert every principle of rational belief, sap the foundations of truth and science, and leave the mind exposed to all the horrors of scepticism."[51] Where there had been certainty, now there was doubt. Where there had been vital purpose, now there was meaninglessness. The promise of Newton—the belief that through rational, scientific enquiry, the mysteries of the universe would be gradually exposed for the service of man and the glory of God—was transformed by Hume into an empty manifestation of intellectual pride. Thus, to virtually every one of Hume's contemporaries, it was inconceivable that he would ever have any disciples. How could he? His passionate rejection of metaphysics at the end of the *Enquiry* was a denial of philosophy itself.

Yet, there was another reason Hume remained a prophet without honor in his own time. His biting attack on the precarious rationalism of the natural theologians might conceivably have served religious purposes; it was

Pascal himself who once said that "proofs convince the mind alone" and that it was "custom," not reason, "which makes so many people Christians, Turks, pagans, artisans, soldiers, and so on." And it was also Pascal who declared that "if a man should do nothing except on the strength of what is certain, he ought to do nothing on that of religion, for it is not certain."[52] In Hume's own century, William Law had indicted all forms of religious rationalism and, in his *Serious Call to a Devout and Holy Life,* summoned men back to the life of deep emotional commitment and pious devotion to the stringent commands of the Gospel. It was not therefore a heretical deviation in the Enlightenment to challenge the persuasive power of formal logic by appealing to the reasons of the heart; skepticism was not the psychological equivalent of religious doubt.

Hume's contemporaries, however, correctly assumed that his reservations about the teleological argument were not those of the fideistic skeptic, not those of the humble man prostrated before the awful incomprehensibility of an all-powerful God. It was perfectly clear from his vicious denunciation of miracles in the *Enquiry,* and from his superbly conceived ironic comparison between Christians and heathens in the *Natural History,* that he was fundamentally antireligious, if not a complete atheist. When John Leland regretted not having included a discussion of Hume in his *View of the Principal Deistical Writers,* published in 1754, it was because he considered him "one of the most subtil writers that had late appeared against Christianity," and solidly in the tradition of the debunking freethinker Thomas Woolston. If there was any question of Hume's intentions, William Warburton answered it in his review of the *Natural History:* Hume, he said, wanted to "establish *Naturalism* on the Ruins of Religion."[53]

Both Leland and Warburton strongly sensed that Hume's philosophy lacked a spiritual dimension and that this lack impoverished his analysis and was largely responsible for the intellectual quarantine placed on his works. Like at least some of his designated adversaries, Hume was broader than he was deep; he never appreciated or fully understood that the foundations of Christianity in the eighteenth century were far more than clever manipulations of the argument from design and that, consequently, to expose the logical inadequacies of that argument, or even to challenge its basic assumptions, was, in a profound sense, to miss the point.

For to recapture the dynamic appeal that natural religion held for countless Enlightenment intellectuals, it is necessary to distinguish between the objects of its thought and the motives which inspired them. The object of natural theology was, of course, to demonstrate rationally the existence of God and to establish by inductive reasoning his chief attributes. The motive behind this exercise, however, was to reconcile both the findings of science and the dictates of reason with the already preexisting emotional and spiritual commitment which practicing Christians felt toward God. In this sense, natural theology was an elaborate religious ritual, long sanctified by tradition, which was the visible and comprehensible expression of an inward, mysterious, and powerful faith. As we shall see with William Paley, few natural theologians were convinced that their carefully articulated arguments would actually persuade anyone to become Christian; they directed their writings to an audience already Christian and whose faith, they hoped, would be reinforced and encouraged by the best arguments human reason could provide.

"Men run with great Avidity to give their Evidence in favour of what flatters their Passions, and their natural Prejudices," Hume wrote in a letter,[54] and it was, paradoxically, one of the major goals of his philosophy to prove why his own arguments would never alter anyone's religious opinions. Yet, for all his emphasis on the importance of "belief" and "custom" in shaping men's minds, it can be argued that he never really understood the distinction between belief, which is based on knowledge and experience, and faith, which involves the total personality in a submission to what Tillich has called an "ultimate concern."

Now the argument from design was a belief in the order and purpose of the universe which Hume, and later Kant, would prove to have no logical foundation; this task, as the modern critics have asserted, was Hume's great triumph. But as long as that belief was only one aspect of a deeper, more immediate personal faith in God, no attack on the argument's premise would convince the theologians that "the cause or causes of order in the universe" bore only "some remote analogy to human intelligence," as Philo argued in the *Dialogues*.[55] This tepid conclusion assumed that men came to God through a tortured process of inductive reasoning. Neither Newton, Berkeley, Joseph Butler, nor Paley had faith in God because he believed the argument from design; they accepted the argument from design because they had faith in God. And as long as this was true for other intellectuals, Hume would remain an isolated figure.

CHAPTER 3

Natural Religion

OF THE HUNDREDS OF NATURAL THEOLOGIES PUBLISHED
in the seventeenth and eighteenth centuries, the overwhelming majority now lie imprisoned and forgotten
in the vaults of great libraries, where they rest as permanent victims of a discredited philosophic tradition. In
the twentieth century, none but the patient scholar would
find intellectual sustenance in the ponderous ruminations
of a Ralph Cudworth or Benjamin Whichcote. The works
and reputations of these pious divines have suffered the
fulfillment of the prophecy which concluded Hume's *Enquiry concerning Human Understanding;* as "sophistry
and illusion," they have felt the "havoc" of subsequent
critics and debunkers.

What condemned natural theology was not its central
question, but the method and assumptions by which that
question was answered. To demonstrate the existence of
God by rational argument struck many observers, even in
the eighteenth century, as a naive exercise in pointlessness
and futility. To the Romantics especially, the "arid" rationalism and "sterile" proofs of Clarke, Butler, and Paley
were the open declaration of a bankrupt religion which
had no faith, a Christianity with its bowels torn away.
"For my part," wrote the skeptical Shelley in the preface
to *Prometheus Unbound,* "I had rather be damned with
Plato and Lord Bacon, than get to heaven with Paley and
Malthus."[1]

This critique by the Romantics has dominated the modern outlook toward eighteenth-century natural religion and it is this same view, frozen into scholarship by the agnostic barbs of Sir Leslie Stephen, which the historian must examine and qualify. There were good reasons, of course, why orthodox divines eschewed an emotional approach to religion in the Enlightenment. A healthy distrust of "enthusiasm" lodged deep in the minds of its most prominent thinkers from Locke through Johnson, not only because such excesses violated their moral and aesthetic sensibilities—their love of balance and decorum—but also because it was this emotionalism which had been directly responsible for the religious intolerance and political upheavals of the seventeenth century. Even Hume, who had no love for natural theology, preferred it to the passionate gloom of the Puritans; and though, with characteristic objectivity, he credited them with diffusing the "spirit of liberty" in the seventeenth century, he was nonetheless mercilessly critical of their fanatic life-styles.[2] For most Enlightenment humanists, enthusiasm was the visible mark of inner self-deception.

Paradoxically, both the orthodox natural theologian and the Dissenting enthusiast shared a common goal: both desired the comfort of certainty for their religious convictions. "We cannot put a greater abuse upon God than to say he is obscure," wrote the Cambridge Platonist Benjamin Whichcote in one of his aphorisms, and Bishop Berkeley, whose *Alciphron* embodied one of the best Christian apologies in the eighteenth century, claimed there to be "no surer mark of prejudice than believing a thing without reason."[3] Unlike the religious enthusiasts, however, natural theologians sought a standard of certainty which lay outside the subjective and misleading dictates of the baser emotions. The appeal of mathematics, for example, lay in its universality, in the intrinsic capacity of its formulas to transcend the limitations of space and time. Euclid's theorems applied to triangles in ancient Greece, as well as to those in rural Dorset.

This appeal was translated into the search for some phenomenon which, like mathematics, was ruled by predictable laws but, unlike mathematics, could be linked directly to the creative power of a Divine Lawgiver. Nature, the raw material of science, satisfied this requirement. If God could not be found in the certainties of Nature, then surely he could not be found in the wavering loyalties of the human heart. It thus became the obligation of every faithful Christian to subject his beliefs to the scrutiny of logic and reason, the tools of science. As Phillip Doddridge put it, "It is certainly the duty of every rational creature to bring his religion to the strictest test, and to return or reject the faith in which he has been educated, as he finds it capable or incapable of rational defence."[4]

For William Paley, the idea of subjecting his faith to a "rational defence" came as early as the 1770s when, as the rector of Appleby, he composed and delivered a series of sermons entitled "The Being of God Demonstrated in the Works of Creation."[5] The notions contained in these sermons served as the metaphysical foundation of both his *Principles,* published in 1785, and his two books on revelation which appeared in the early 1790s. In effect, the argument from design was the intellectual armature of his entire philosophy, and by the late 1790s, he recognized the need to develop this argument in a more systematic fashion. The result was the *Natural Theology,* published in 1802.

As was true of the *Evidences,* the *Natural Theology* was a magnificently written work. Its argument began with the opening sentence and continued, uninterrupted, for almost four hundred pages. There were no unnecessary digressions and few eccentricities of style. He marshaled his evidence to fit his argument and usually admitted when it did not. He had an almost uncanny feel for the possible attacks of his critics and intercepted their objections before they overwhelmed his argument. His replies were sensitive and penetrating. It can be said without exaggeration that Paley's *Natural Theology* provides the most consistent and searching statement of the teleological argument in the English language. The failures of the book are those of the argument, not of Paley. It is, and deserves to be, a philosophic classic.

For convenience, the *Natural Theology* can be divided into three major sections, each of which provides an entry into the mind of Paley and the intellectual traditions which it absorbed. In the opening section—roughly the first six chapters—Paley stated the argument of the book and attempted to refute the objections of his occasionally skeptical audience. In part two, which encompassed the middle seventeen chapters and formed the bulk of the book, he presented a lengthy sampling of the scientific evidence which buttressed his argument. Finally, in part three, he discussed the attributes of God and addressed himself to the vexing problem of evil.

II

In its most primitive form, the fundamental argument of natural religion can be reduced to the following syllogism:

Major Premise: Nature everywhere exhibits elements of purpose and design.

Minor Premise: Design must always be the product of a designer.

Conclusion: Nature is the product of a designer [who is God].

In their lengthy and often tedious expositions, most natural theologians channeled their energies into substantiating the major premise; the vast reservoir of newly acquired scientific data made it the easiest to prove, and it obviously penetrated to the core of the problem. Thus, for example, in their enormously popular natural theologies, both John Ray and his disciple William Derham focused their attention on the glories and wonders of nature, ignoring any direct statement of the minor premise, which they implicitly assumed was beyond dispute.[6] Though, like most natural theologians of the Enlightenment, both Ray and Derham organized their scientific material into a comprehensible pattern, they never discussed the teleological argument itself in any thorough or coherent fashion, and it was not until David Hume trained his sights on the argument in the *Dialogues* that it attained the prominence of serious debate.

The opening six chapters of Paley's *Natural Theology* thus became the first systematic presentation of the teleological argument in the eighteenth century. The hallmark of this discussion and the conceptual center of gravity for the entire discourse was, of course, the famous opening pages where Paley compared finding a stone to finding a watch:

> In crossing a heath, suppose I pitched my foot against a *stone*, and were asked how the stone came to be there: I might possibly answer, that, for any thing I knew to the contrary, it had lain there for ever; nor would it perhaps be very easy to show the absurdity of this answer. But suppose I had found a *watch* upon the ground, and it should be inquired how the watch happened to be in that place; I should hardly think of the answer which I had before given,—that, for any thing I knew, the watch might have always been there. . . . For when we come to inspect the watch, we perceive (what we could not discover in the stone) that its several parts are framed and put together for a purpose, *e.g.*, that they are so formed and adjusted as to produce motion, and that motion so regulated as to point out the hour of the day; . . . .The inference we think is inevitable, that the watch must have had a maker: that there must have existed, at some time, and at some place or other, an artificer or artificers who formed it for the purpose which we find it actually to answer: who comprehended its construction, and designed its use.[7]

Paley was establishing here the first two terms of what would become his central analogy; that is, a watch is to a watchmaker as nature is to God. The argument's major premise thus involved proving that the workings of nature were closely comparable to the mechanism of a watch—a comparison which consumed most of the book—and the minor premise asserted that God was not unlike a mighty watchmaker, though it was on this presumed similarity that the question of proportionality became especially acute.

The sources of this comparison stretched into antiquity. In his *De natura Deorum*, Cicero has his spokesman, Balbus, compare the world to a "sun dial or a water clock" and later praise the craftsman who created the "incredibly numerous and inexhaustibly varied" species of nature.[8] Yet it was not until the seventeenth century that the watch analogy became the obvious, even trite, metaphor for the hitherto mysterious operations of nature. In particular, the complex and subtle intricacies of the famous Strasbourg clock provided both scientist and theologian with an obvious analogue for what they were uncovering about God's world; and for a theological scientist like Robert Boyle, ever alert for the dramatic simile which would appeal to untutored readers, it became a favorite comparison which he invoked frequently throughout his works.[9]

The usually cited source for Paley's watch analogy was Bernard Nieuwentyt, the Dutch theologian whose three-volume *Religious Philosopher* was translated and published in England in 1719. Early in the first volume, Nieuwentyt imagined the reaction of a man who, cast "in a desert or solitary Place, where few People are used to pass," would suddenly stumble upon a "Watch, shewing the Hours, Minutes, and Days of the month."[10] He then developed the analogy along conventional lines. In both structure and phraseology, Paley leaned heavily on the little parable of this meticulous Dutchman; and yet, there remained one major difference between the two versions. For Nieuwentyt, the watch analogy did not occupy center stage in his overall production; it played only a minor role and was included, almost casually, as a useful illustration of a larger, more dramatic principle. For Paley, the watch became the controlling motif of his entire book.

The first and most obvious characteristic of this motif was its assumption of a mechanistic nature, its belief that nature ticked like a clock. "Our business is with mechanism" (p. 232), wrote Paley in one of his chapters, and in conforming to this standard, he naturally turned to those areas of science which conveniently fitted his model. Thus the lion's share of the *Natural Theology* revolved around an extended and learned discussion of human and animal anatomy, surely the best example of mechanism in nature. "For my part," he observed, "I take my stand in human anatomy; and the examples of mechanism . . . from the copious catalogue which it supplies" (p. 372).

This mechanistic assumption, however, imposed awkward limitations on the range and depth of Paley's excursion into natural philosophy. It meant that some scientific disciplines could not be related to the general argument or were applicable only tangentially. Thus, Paley made it clear at the beginning of his chapter on astronomy that "it is *not* the best medium through which to prove the agency of an intelligent Creator," though it does manifest "the magnificence of his operations" (p. 263). In a similar manner, chemistry, which lagged behind the other sciences in the Enlightenment, could not "afford the same species of argument as that which mechanism affords" (p. 58) and thereby eroded the claims for universality which confident teleologists like to presume. Of eighteenth-century natural theologians, Paley was perhaps the most geared toward mechanism, and this proclivity, which released his talents as a brilliant explicator of complex scientific detail, also straitjacketed his efforts as a Christian apologist. Like all comparisons, both scientific and literary, the watch analogy collapsed if pressed too far.

An example of this occurred early in the book. The major premise of Paley's teleological argument was that in its structure and operations, nature was similar to a watch. Yet nature holds the unique power of reproduction and generation, a power not inherent in a watch. This dissimilarity forced Paley to stretch his metaphor and ask the reader to assume that the watch he found while crossing a heath "possessed the unexpected property of producing, in the course of its movement, another watch like itself" (p. 6). Paley thought it "conceivable" but must have sensed that this early in the development of his argument, such a hypothesis injured his credibility.

Yet, it was not critical that his audience sincerely believe in the generative powers of an imaginary watch, since the whole purpose of the illustration was to create a hypothetical model which, not unlike a legal fiction, was a pure and unencumbered standard from which to understand, measure, and judge reality as men actually experienced it. To this extent, the watch analogy was similar to the various state of nature theories popular with political philosophers. Its function was to explain the origin and purpose of the phenomenon under discussion by forcing the reader to shed his dogmatic preconceptions about the subject and thereby view it from a fresh perspective. Paley wanted his readers to examine nature like a man who, while walking along a heath, suddenly discovered at his feet something completely new and quite extraordinary—a mechanical device which told the time. In one sense, then, whether or not the properties of the watch strictly conformed to the characteristics of nature became irrelevant.

What the man would discover about the watch was, of course, that its entire mechanism was devised for the practical purpose of indicating the time of day, "that, if the different parts had been differently shaped from what they are, of a different size from what they are . . . either no motion at all would have carried on in the machine, or none which would have answered the use that is now served by it" (pp. 1–2). But to arrive at this elementary conclusion, it was necessary for the man to examine the watch carefully, lest he believe it operated because of some occult power or by magic. Thus the second characteristic of Paley's major argument for the existence of God was its thoroughgoing empiricism. To prove that the structure of various creatures in nature was, like a watch, designed for a specific purpose could be neither intuited nor deduced without concrete evidence. The proboscis attached to the head of a butterfly could not be explained by sitting alone with a pencil in an oak-paneled room; you needed the butterfly. For the teleological argument to succeed, it was first necessary to compile a significant number of observations which showed that the individual parts of nature worked together for specific ends; that, like the mainspring of a watch, the proboscis was *telic*.

Paley was thus building a probability argument grounded on the conformity of his empirical evidence to a central analogy. Its theoretical foundation had been laid by Bishop Butler, whose *Analogy of Religion* contained the most extensive and searching discussion of analogical reasoning in the century. Butler saw that the method of analogies was "to join abstract reasoning with the observation of facts"; analogies argued comparatively from likeness to likeness, from part to whole, and from the present to the future. But at best, they could only establish probability. Now the difference between demonstrative and probable reasoning, said the Bishop, was only a matter of degree; and consequently it was possible for something of initially low presumption, if observed frequently enough, to attain nearly the level of certainty. It depended, of course, "on the degree and exactness of the whole

analogy or likeness," but, since man's faculties were limited, we must accept arguments of high probability as
sufficient, as "the very guide of life."[11]

In *Natural Theology*, Paley devoted much of his energy
to bolstering the probability of his basic analogy. Yet, in an
interesting departure from Butler's argument, he claimed
that his evidence was by no means interdependent, that
each illustration of design could stand alone as a necessary
and sufficient confirmation of God's existence.

> The proof is not a conclusion which lies at the end of a chain
> of reasoning, of which chain each instance of contrivance is
> only a link, and of which, if one link fail, the whole falls; but it
> is an argument separately supplied by every separate exam-
> ple. An error in stating an example, affects only that example.
> The argument is cumulative, in the fullest sense of that term.
> The eye proves it without the ear; the ear without the eye.
> The proof in each example is complete; for when the design
> of the part, and the conduciveness of its structure to that
> design is shown, the mind may set itself at rest; no future
> consideration can detract any thing from the force of the
> example. [Pp. 53–54]

This statement was partly an eloquent refusal to engage
in the tortured deductive logic of such English rationalists
as Samuel Clarke, who valiantly endeavored to demonstrate God's existence through a series of interlocking
deductions. Paley was too much the empiricist to rally
under that banner. On the other hand, he was also un-
willing to abide by the exacting criteria of empirical
science. To the scientist, a single piece of evidence would
be a necessary but not a sufficient validation of a disputed
theorem. As a theologian, however—and as a master rhet-
orician—Paley could defiantly assert that a lone illustration of design in nature fulfilled his expectations, that the
structure of an eye or an ear, for example, was enough
evidence to banish the skepticism of a doubting Thomas.

Yet before he could proceed with the scores of examples which he accumulated—each sufficient in his view to confirm his thesis—one critical task remained. The minor premise of his essay was that like a watchmaker, God was the master craftsman of the entire universe. But was this the only possibility? Was it not conceivable that ordered and purposeful natural contrivances originated in something other than an omnipotent Creator? Might they not, for example, be the product of chance, as some of the ancients once maintained? Sensitive to these questions and confident of his ability to refute the counterproposals suggested by skeptics both on the Continent and in Britain, Paley analyzed what he considered the five major alternate theories for the origin of the universe.

The first of these was the easiest to dismiss. That the elements of design in nature were "no proof of contrivance," but "only a motive to induce the mind to think so" (p. 5) had been Hume's "subjectivist" position and the one which, when advanced by Bishop Berkeley, had prompted Samuel Johnson to kick a stone in refutation. Paley thought it patent nonsense and spent little time on it, pausing only to register "surprize" that anyone would entertain such folly. As a philosopher, he routinely accepted the existence of an objective reality outside the mind and was far too practical to be buried in obscure metaphysics. By his hasty refusal even to discuss the problem, he repudiated the notion that such questions were valid subjects for philosophic analysis.

He was equally impatient with the view that the world was the product of a chance combination of atoms. This belief had been the favorite target of earlier natural theologies, particularly in the seventeenth century when the slim volumes of Epicurus became a major battleground for crusading divines such as the Cambridge Platonists.[12] Like these earlier combatants, Paley attempted to rout the argument with uncharacteristic contempt and derision: "What does chance ever do for us?" he asked early in the essay; "In the human body, for instance, chance, *i.e.* the operation of causes without design, may produce a wen, a wart, a mole, a pimple, but never an eye." For Paley, the structure and careful intertwinings of virtually everything in nature were simply too complicated to be fobbed off as the chance concoction of a meaningless whirl of atoms. The probability was too low, and experience against it. "I desire no greater certainty in reasoning," he asserted confidently, "than that by which chance is excluded from the present disposition of the natural world" (p.44).

A third alternative explanation to the teleological argument centered on the view that order and design were the product of laws or scientific principles, which dictated the physical structure of natural phenomenon and described their behavior. Under this view, there was no ultimate lawgiver, only laws themselves. Paley considered this explanation completely inadequate; to claim a "law" caused anything perverted language and harkened back to the "occult qualities" of medieval theology. Law presupposed an agent without which "the *law* does nothing, is nothing" (p. 5). Moreover, nature is not universally ordered, as it would be if it were acting under a blind principle. It is ordered only when some purpose is served; thus the eye has a certain necessary structure; whereas most geological formations do not, since "no useful purpose would have arisen from moulding rocks and mountains into regular solids." To explain the origin and workings of the universe by appealing to some scientific law or vague "principle of order" constituted "a mere substitution of words for reasons, names for causes" (p. 49).

But there was a fourth, more cogent explanation, raised by Hume in his *Dialogues,* which accounted for design in nature without dredging up the slippery problem of ultimate origins. Philo maintained that natural theologians committed what logicians call "the fallacy of composition"; that is, because everything in the universe must have a cause, therefore the universe itself must have a cause. In effect, this was similar to arguing that because every member of the group has a mother, therefore the group has a mother. This reasoning was false because the group, like the universe, was of a logically different class than each of its constituents and consequently statements applicable to one were not necessarily applicable to the other. Since no man has witnessed worlds coming into being, no one can discuss properly the universe as a composite unit; it lies beyond the reach of human experience.[13]

Without mentioning Hume by name, Paley countered this objection by denying that the universe was of a distinct logical class and therefore beyond causal explanations.

> Where there is a tendency, or, as we increase the number of terms, a continual approach towards a limit, *there*, by supposing the number of terms to be what is called infinite, we may conceive the limit to be attained: but where there is no such tendency or approach, nothing is effected by lengthening the series. There is no difference as to the point in question (whatever there may be as to many points) between one series and another; between a series which is finite and a series which is infinite. A chain, composed of an infinite number of links, can no more support itself, than a chain composed of a finite number of links. [P. 9]

With his usual penetration, Paley perceived that Hume's appeal to the fallacy of composition—his implicit reliance on infinite regress—was less an answer to the question of the universe's origin than a repudiation of the question itself. And as long as Paley could assume that the only difference between a finite and infinite series was a matter of length and that, moreover, causality was like a me-

chanical sequence, he effectively stifled Philo's objections.[14] Thus, at the precise moment his teleological argument encountered a reasoned objection, Paley could
appeal to the cosmological explanation, which, as Kant
maintained, lay behind it. Infinite regress begged the critical question of first cause; it acknowledged contrivance
but failed to provide a contriver; it admitted design but
could find no designer. As a body of explanation, it lacked a
head.

These objections did not apply to the fifth major alternative which might have endangered the minor premise of
Paley's teleological argument. When he composed the
Natural Theology in the opening years of the nineteenth
century, the theory of evolution was still in embryonic
form; adherents such as Buffon were convinced that the
intricate mosaic of biological life was the product of an
extended and continuous historical development, but they
lacked a mechanism, an explanatory model, which accounted for the disappearance of some species and the
vigorous survival of others.[15] Paley was not blind to the
threat these theories posed to his own account of the origin
of the universe; the argument from design most common
to the Enlightenment assumed that God forged the universe in one dramatically creative stroke, and though this
portrayal of the earth's beginning coincided with the biblical narrative in Genesis, it excluded all but minor developments subsequent to that one great week of immortal
labor. As a theory of origin, natural theology locked itself
out of history.

Paley classed evolutionary theories into two distinct
categories. The first, which he considered derivative of the
chance hypothesis, claimed that "every organized body
which we see, are only so many out of the possible varieties
and combinations of being, which the lapse of infinite ages
has brought into existence" and that millions of other
species perished, "being by the defect of their constitution

incapable of preservation, or of continuance by generation" (p. 44). Paley attacked this argument by calling up
the strongest weapon in his arsenal; there existed, he said,
no empirical evidence to prove such a theory. "We should
see unicorns and mermaids, sylphs and centaurs, the
fancies of painters, and the fables of poets" if this
conjecture were true. Instead, nature manifests an orderly
division of plants and animals into genera and species
which, by its rationality and design, contradicts an arbitrary selection process. More important, since the theory
offers no explanation "why, if these deperdits ever existed,
they have now disappeared," it can remain only the clever
conjecture of an idle mind (p. 45). In this accusation, Paley
pinpointed what would remain the major weakness of the
evolutionists down to *The Origin of Species.*

In describing the second type of evolutionary theory,
Paley came perilously close to providing the mechanism
which would eventually clinch the triumph of historical
biology. "That the parts were not intended for the use, but
that the use arose out of the parts" struck Paley as an
"intelligible" distinction (p. 47). Clearly the fact that a
cabinetmaker polishes wood with a fish skin does not mean
that the fish skin was designed specifically for cabinet-
makers. The concept of final cause can be easily abused.
Yet, Paley maintained that such an illustration cannot be
imposed on nature for the simple reason that the intelligence and volition involved in the cabinetmaker's choosing a suitably rough fish skin with which to rub wood has
little or no analogy in the behavior of plants and animals.
"None of the senses fundamentally depend upon the
election of the animal, consequently neither upon his sa-
gacity, nor his experience." Paley freely admitted that
there were instances where "organization seems to determine the habits of the animal, and its choice to a
particular mode of life"; but in all these cases the structures bear a close relation to the animal's environment,

over which it exercises no control. Thus, in cross-examining an imaginary evolutionist, Paley asked: "The web-foot determines, you say, the duck to swim; but what would that avail, if there were no water to swim in?" (pp. 47–49). For Paley, the critical factor remained volition; only if a physical change or behavioral pattern stemmed from the active will and intelligence of the animal would it be proper to say that the use arose out of the parts. Men did not discover they had eyes and then saw; they saw and then knew that they had eyes.

Paley returned to the theory of evolution later in the essay, this time calling it the system of *"appentencies"* and offering an example which, because of his customary objectivity in relating the arguments of his opponents, now strikes the reader as mildly prescient.

> A piece of animated matter, for example, that was endued with a propensity to *fly* . . . would, in a course of ages, if not in a million of years (for our theorists, having eternity to dispose of, are never sparing in time), acquire *wings*. The same tendency to loco-motion in an aquatic animal, or rather in an animated lump, which might happen to be surrounded by water, would end in the production of *fins:* in a living substance, confined to the solid earth, would put out *legs* and *feet*; or, if it took a different turn, would break the body into ringlets, and conclude by *crawling* upon the ground.[P. 300]

To counter these conjectures, Paley again appeals to the evidence. Yes, he admits, the pouch of a pelican may have arisen from its storing of food over an extended period of time, but "how comes it to pass, that the pelican alone was the inventress, and her descendants the only inheritors, of this curious resource?" Moreover, there are numerous parts of the body where structure could not have been formed by habit, no matter what the time span. Blood cannot help form the valves which convey it and "no effort of the animal could determine the clothing of its skin." In short, when applied to nature, the system of appentencies "is contradicted by many of the phenomena, and totally inadequate to others" (pp. 304–6).

Paley does not burden the evolutionists, however, with the charge of atheism; unlike many of the defenders of the teleological argument later in the nineteenth century, he saw no necessary conflict between a faith in God and a belief in evolution. Yet, in one critical area, these two allegiances clashed; by claiming that use developed from parts, the evolutionists, Paley asserted, banished final causes from their natural philosophy and thereby dispensed with "the necessity, in each particular case, of an intelligent, designing mind, for the contriving and determining of the forms which organized bodies bear" (p. 301). This omission might have meant, for example, that the present form and future development of natural life followed no master plan, or controlling *telos,* thus casting men adrift in a meaningless world. Without final cause, God became an impotent spectator of the contest for survival.

It would be easy to indulge in anachronism and condemn Paley's reflections on evolution as naive and irrelevant. His assumption that design always implied a designer and his insistence that volition must initiate the process of change would eventually be swept away and forgotten by both scientists and philosophers. Yet, for all its errors in judgment, Paley's reply to the evolutionists, like his rebuttal of Hume's *Dialogues,* stands as one of the most thoughtful and searching in the nineteenth century. Unlike some of his earlier contemporaries in the Scottish Common Sense school, he was fair to the arguments of his adversaries and rarely avoided serious confrontation by lapsing into ridicule. And, as in his response to the charge that the argument from design committed the fallacy of composition, his logic and penetration often challenge our own prejudices and stock ideas. For, as many philosophers have recognized, Hume did not refute the teleological argument; he merely rejected as unanswerable the question behind it.[16]

The statement of Paley's central argument was now complete. He had established the watch analogy and responded to his critics on the possible alternatives to his minor premise that God was similar to a watchmaker. Only his major premise now wanted proof; and it was here that Paley seized the offensive. He would not only prove that nature was like the solitary watch of the opening chapter, he would demonstrate that "the contrivances of nature surpass the contrivances of art, in the complexity, subtilty, and curiosity of the mechanism; and still more, if possible, do they go beyond them in number and variety" (p. 12).

III

To prove that nature is similar to a watch—that its individual parts were so contrived as to work together for a common end—Paley laid before the reader five major characteristics of plant and animal anatomy which strongly suggested the imprint of a guiding hand. The first of these specific proofs focused on structural adaptions within an organism, that is, the internal anatomical adjustments which permit it to function with maximum efficiency and harmony. Thus, for example, he appeals at length to the wonders of bilateral symmetry, noting with evident satisfaction the balance and congruity between the two sides of any animal. "It is the most difficult thing that can be to get a wig made even," he exclaimed in reference to mortal craftsmen, "yet how seldom is the *face* awry!" (p. 129). Moreover, when one examines the inner organs of these same animals, this symmetry, which is no longer necessary, no longer exists, thus proving "that the external proportion does not arise from any equality in the shape or pressure of the internal contents" (p. 131), as the evolutionists maintained. Finally, he rejoices in what he calls the "package" of animal mass; how, with all its internal intricacies and operations—heart, lungs, bowels, liver—the entire body functions virtually unhindered under exertion and stress. A circus tumbler inverts and contorts his body without any damaging effect to his digestion or blood circulation.

Second, Paley detects the mark of a great architect in the various structural adaptions of animals to their environment.

> Whenever we find a general plan pursued, yet with such variations in it, as are, in each case, required by the particular exigency of the subject to which it is applied, we possess, in such a plan and such adaptation, the strongest evidence that can be afforded of intelligence and design; an evidence which the most completely excludes every other hypothesis. If the general plan proceeded from any fixed necessity in the nature of things, how could it accommodate itself to the various wants and uses which it had to serve under different circumstances, and on different occasions? [Pp. 146–47]

The outer covering of animals always suits their particular environment; those which live in colder climates are protected by thick fur, whereas birds, which live in warmer climates, have light, smooth feathers that are uniquely designed for aerial maneuvering. "Can it be doubted," Paley inquires in a later chapter where he resumes the same theme, "whether the *wings of birds* bear a relation to air, and the *fins of fish* to water?" (p. 203). Then too, the compatible relationship between sleep and night provides another illustration of how animals are designed to relate comfortably to their environment. "Night brings with it a silence, and a cessation of activity, which allows of sleep being taken without interruption, and without loss," notes Paley, and he concludes, "Animal existence is made up of action and slumber; nature has provided a season for each." Since day and night stem from the earth's position in relation to the sun, nightly slumber "connects the meanest individual with the universe itself; a chicken roosting upon its perch, with the sphere revolving in the firmament" (pp. 205–7).

Third, within the kaleidoscopic variety of nature a number of animals possess structural peculiarities which bear no close analogue in other creatures. Thus, for example, "the oil with which *birds* prune their feathers and the organ which supplies it, is a specific provision for the winged creation" (p. 169). In a similar manner, the air bladder of a fish affords a clear example of a mechanical apparatus which permits it to change its swimming depth by regulating its specific gravity. "Nothing similar to the air bladder is found in land animals," Paley interjects, and then, in a calculated swipe at the evolutionists, continues: "Life in the water has no natural tendency to produce a bag of air. Nothing can be farther from an acquired organization than this is" (p. 171). In his other examples—the fang of a viper, the bag of the opossum, the camel's stomach, the beak of a woodpecker—he continues to underscore the same fundamental principle; these anatomical oddities which ensure survival in hostile surroundings could only have been the product of design; they could not have arisen spontaneously from their environment; they must have been created for these specific purposes.

This same logic holds true for what Paley calls "prospective contrivances," or cases where nature provides an animal with equipment that remains inactive until the time it is needed.

> The human teeth afford an instance, not only of prospective contrivance, but of the completion of the contrivance being designedly suspended. They are formed within the gums, and there they stop; the fact being, that their farther advance to

maturity would not only be useless to the new-born animal, but extremely in its way; . . . .By the time they are wanted, the teeth are ready. . . . Nature, namely, that intelligence which was employed in creation, looked beyond the first year of the infant's life. [Pp. 175–76]

Another illustration of this careful preparation for the future can be found in a mother's milk, which is generated only at the precise time when the baby animal comes into the world. To Paley, "the lacteal system is a constant wonder: and it adds to other causes of our admiration, that the number of teats or paps in which species is found to bear a proportion to the number of young" (p. 178).

Fifth and finally, there are those contrivances which are compensatory; that is, cases where "the *defects* of one part, or of one organ, are supplied by the structure of another part, or of another organ" (pp. 191–92). Here Paley lists a number of interesting examples: cranes cannot swim because they lack web feet, yet they have long legs for wading; the spider cannot fly after its winged prey, therefore it traps them in a web; the eyes of insects cannot revolve in their sockets, yet by means of an internal prism they catch all the light at once; animals which have no teeth ruminate their food instead; others which lack feet have another mechanism with which to crawl. In all these cases—which Paley outlines in detail—the particular compensating structures "exhibit a specimen, not only of design (which is attested by the advantage), but of consummate art, and, as I may say, of elaborate preparation in accomplishing that design" (p. 193).

Though Paley stressed he was "not writing a system of natural history" (p. 222), he manifested in his *Natural Theology* a remarkably broad knowledge of Enlightenment science. He gleaned this information from essentially three sources: first, from a variety of published material both scientific and theological; second, from the contributions of scientific friends who saw in his work a significant attempt to place their factual information into a solid theological context; and finally, from personal observations recorded during his frequent excursions into the surrounding countryside. It was from these raw materials that Paley forged the major premise of his argument.

Of the published sources, the great preponderance were scientific treatises or texts of experiments, ranging from Colin Maclaurin's superb popularization of Newton to "Dr. Hunter's Account of the Dissection of a Whale."[17] As might be expected, Paley relied heavily on the work of anatomists, especially those of Alexander Monro, James Keil, and William Cheselden. Cheselden, whose *Anatomy of the Human Body* Paley cited more than any other single source, was generally acknowledged as the best British surgeon and anatomist in the eighteenth century. The intimate friend of Pope and Newton, and physician to Queen Caroline, he was a man who, in his own estimate, possessed "a mind that never ruffled."[18] The *Anatomy*, published in 1713, drew praise for its concise descriptions and ran through thirteen editions in a few years. No doubt appreciative of his lucidity, Paley departed from Cheselden only to impose the proper religious gloss on the otherwise neutral information.

Paley also borrowed some of his facts from other natural theologians, notably John Ray and William Derham. Derham, who began his career as a country clergyman and finished it as head of St. John's College, Oxford, delivered the Boyle lectures in 1711, and published shortly thereafter his *Astro-Theology* and the enormously popular *Physico-Theology*. This latter work, designed to be "acceptable to Young Gentlemen at the Universities," contained no direct statement of the teleological argument, though of course it employed telic reasoning extensively. Paley freely borrowed from it material on the vision of birds, the digestive system, and, in what may have become one of his two arguments for God's benevolence, on the "Delight which the various Tribes of Animals have to the Varieties of Food."[19] As always, he condensed this source, distilling fifty pages of Derham's turgid prose into five pages of lucid analysis.

When Paley exhausted published sources, he could consult his scientific friends such as John Brinkley, the first Astronomer Royal for Ireland. Like Paley, Brinkley was also a graduate of Cambridge and had been Senior Wrangler in 1788. A brilliant student and later a popular lecturer, Brinkley became Andrew Professor of Astronomy at the University of Dublin in 1792 and, as a friend of John Law, met Paley shortly thereafter. Though Paley did not think astronomy "the best medium through which to prove the agency of an intelligent Creator" (p. 263) he wanted to include in his analysis an informed discussion of this critical field, and Brinkley happily offered to provide one. The result was chapter 22 of the *Natural Theology*, which Brinkley composed almost in its entirety. Claiming among other things that God created and regulated centripetal forces, Brinkley filled a vacuum in Paley's knowledge which he gracefully acknowledged in an opening footnote (p. 263n).

The third and final source of Paley's scientific information was his own personal observation during his prolonged and often intensive study of the surrounding countryside. As his son tells us, "he used to take from his own table to his study the back-bone of a hare, or the pinion of a fowl," and on returning from his frequent forays into the country, he would often "pull out of his pocket a stone or a plant to illustrate what he had himself found, or seen advanced by others without sufficient minuteness."[20] The wild beauties of Cumberland and Westmorland provided an unrivaled opportunity for such field expeditions, an opportunity which he felt compensated for the intellectual isolation of the region. As he told the young clergy of Carlisle:

> The deepest and most secluded recesses of our mountains are the best fitted for the researches I am recommending; and he who does not turn his mind to the subject when he finds himself placed in the midst of a magnificent museum, not only neglects an opportunity of rational recreation, but neglects the best thing, in some cases perhaps the only good thing, which his situation affords.[21]

This interest in nature dovetailed with his work as a theologian; he demonstrated in the *Natural Theology* an almost professional ability to describe and analyze the intricate machinations of his natural environment.

All his life Paley was a man fundamentally interested in how things worked. As a child in Giggleswick, he enjoyed observing local craftsmen at their trade, "and he used not seldom to sit up all night with one of his neighbours to watch the process of soap-boiling." Considered remarkable for the shrewdness of his observations as a youth, Paley carried this inquisitiveness with him throughout his life. In a revealing letter to J. D. Carlyle in 1799, he actually made a list of details he wanted Carlisle to supply as he made his way through the Middle East.

> 2. Give us one day at Constantinople minutely from morning to night; what you do, see, eat, and hear.
>
> 3. Let us know what the common people have to dinner; get, if you can, a peasant's actual dinner and bottle; for instance, if you see a man working the field, call to him to bring the dinner he has with him, and describe it minutely. . . .
>
> 7. Get into the inside of a cottage, describe furniture, utensils, what you find actually doing. . . .[22]

These questions, unusual in a personal letter to an old friend, manifest a curiosity about the minutiae of life which proved especially useful when he turned his mind to the complexities of natural philosophy.

For, as an explicator of natural religion, Paley was far more engaging than many of his venerable predecessors. He chose only "the most striking and best understood" examples from natural history and admirably refrained from cluttering his book with technical language. As always, he wrote clearly. Working without the benefit of plates and figures, he encapsulated in a short paragraph the essence of an anatomical structure and delivered it to the readers in palatable form. More important, he approached his subject with a childlike awe and bubbling exuberance which enliven his descriptions—and often unintentionally provide the only humor in the book. Witness his famous analysis of the human throat, a description which one scholar has called the "devotional hymn to the epiglottis."[23]

> Reflect how frequently we swallow, how constantly we breathe. In a city-feast, for example, what deglutition, what annelation! yet does this little cartilage, the epiglottis, so effectually interpose its office, so securely guard the entrance of the wind-pipe, that whilst morsel after morsel, draught after draught, are coursing one another over it, an accident of a crumb or a drop slipping into this passage (which nevertheless must be opened for the breath every second of time), excites in the whole company, not only alarm by its danger, but surprize by its novelty. Not two guests are choked in a century. [P. 124]

There is no reason to doubt Paley's sincerity in composing this passage. As a theologian fascinated by the discoveries and observations of natural philosophers, he was continually stunned by the beauty and efficiency of nature. If his occasional flights into hyperbole strike the modern reader as ludicrous, they were nevertheless the reflection of an intense appreciation of God's creation.

It was to describing the attributes of this God that Paley devoted the last portion of his essay. Certainly the obvious implication of the teleological argument was that God was similar to a grand and great watchmaker—a contriver of enormous skill and wisdom. Yet did this mean that once having completed his universe, God removed himself from Creation; that he was a distant and indifferent Deity whom men respected but could not fear, admired but did not love? After all, the man who found the watch while crossing the heath never actually saw the watchmaker; he could only infer, somewhat feebly, that once some individual, somewhere, crafted the wonderful mechanism he now held in his hand.

It is commonplace to say that eighteenth-century natural theologians approached the great problems of religious discourse in a practical, even pedestrian manner; that, unlike Pascal or, ironically, even Hume, they did not enter the gates of higher theology with fear and trembling or a pronounced sense that describing an omniscient and incomprehensible Deity was, ipso facto, a contradiction in terms, a dilemma incapable of being resolved into an acceptable paradox or a dialectical truth. It is also said of natural religion that it banished God from the universe; that in narrowing his influence and power to the initial act of creation, it removed God from the daily activities of the world and relegated him to the lesser role of a benevolent observer. Thus, on the one hand, it is argued the Enlightenment theologians in England worshiped an immanent and familiar God, while on the other hand it is claimed that these same divines created a transcendent and unknown Deity. This inconsistency suggests a misunderstanding of natural theology which may be resolved by examining the pertinent reflections of Paley, one of the best expositors of the entire group.

Paley devoted the final hundred pages of his *Natural Theology* to delineating the attributes of God. He acknowledged that the "great difficulty" of such a task was that no one has ever actually seen God, and that his existence lies outside the realm of sensory verification. At the same time, however, no one has ever seen gravity and yet no one doubts its existence. We have knowledge of many forces only by their effects and, in a loosely analogous way, God is one of them. Though it is impossible to describe him with complete precision, some things about his personality are clear (pp. 286–87).

In using the word "personality," Paley employed a notion of divinity that was blatantly anthropomorphic; and yet within the logic of the teleological argument, the term seemed inescapable. The works of nature implied an intelligent creator; and intelligence was always the product of mind.

> Now that which can contrive, which can design, must be a person. These capacities constitute personality, for they imply consciousness and thought. They require that which can perceive an end or purpose; as well as the power of providing means, and of directing them to their end. They require a centre in which perceptions unite, and from which volitions flow; which is mind. The acts of a mind prove the existence of a mind; and in whatever a mind resides, is a person. The seat of intellect is a person. [P. 284]

God is self-sufficient and self-sustaining, and in this ability to have existed without the prior exertion of another, more powerful Being lay the critical distinction between the personality of God and that of mortal men. The human personality is the product of many forces, many desires; only God is First Cause. Moreover, unlike the anthropomorphic deities which ruled the mythologies of the ancient world, the God of natural religion was not the larger shadow of the men who worshiped him, but incorporated only certain qualities of those men. Unlike Zeus or Mars or Apollo, he was neither proud, nor wrathful, nor jealous. Rather, he was without base emotions, since they would be unworthy of him. He was the ultimate embodiment of the distinguishing characteristic between men and animals; he was Pure Mind (pp. 285–89).

Of the conventional roll call of superlatives generally attributed to God—omnipotence, omniscience, omnipresence, etc.—Paley considers in depth only two: his unity and his goodness. The unity of the Deity was stressed almost as a matter of form, since to any rational theologian of the eighteenth century it was axiomatic that God was a logically unified, utterly consistent being. It was contrary to the principles of reason to portray a God who acted contradictorily, though early in the century Leibniz had accused Samuel Clarke of creating just such a God.[24] To defeat any similar accusations against his own system, Paley appealed directly to the uniformity of nature; "In truth," he argued, "the same order of things attends us, wherever we go. The elements act upon one another, electricity operates, the tides rise and fall, the magnetic needle elects its position, in one region of the earth and sea, as well as in another" (p. 313). This unity of law and natural behavior pointed toward the unified Deity who created it; the visible reflected the invisible.

It was from observations of nature that Paley also inferred God's goodness, an attribute of crucial importance which he proved by means of two interlocking propositions. The first asserted that "in a vast plurality of instances in which contrivance is perceived, the design of the contrivance is *beneficial*" (p. 316). It would be this premise, gleaned from the rich harvest of empirical proof that he had laid before the reader in the preceding section of the essay, which became the chief sustenance of his vigorous optimism. Paley harbored an intense, subjective belief that nature was alive with joy.

> It is a happy world after all. The air, the earth, the water, teem with delighted existence. In a spring noon, or a summer evening, on whichever side I turn my eyes, myriads of happy beings crowd upon my view. "The insect youth are on the wing." Swarms of new-born *flies* are trying their pinions in

the air. Their sportive motions, their wanton mazes, their gratuitous activity, their continual change of place without use or purpose, testify their joy, and the exultation which they felt in their lately discovered faculties. . . . Other species are *running about*, with an alacrity in their motions, which carries with it every mark of pleasure. Large patches of ground are sometimes half covered with these brisk and sprightly natures. If we look to what the *waters* produce, shoals of the fry of fish frequent the margins of rivers, of lakes, and of the sea itself. These are so happy, that they know not what to do with themselves. [Pp. 317–18]

In many ways this is a breathtaking quotation, for in it Paley manifested an anthropomorphic conception of nature more akin to the nascent pantheism of Wordsworth than to the objective, lifeless universe which Newton subjected to the abstract formulas of mathematics and which has come to dominate our textbook view of Enlightenment science and theology. Far from being the "dull affair, soundless, scentless, colourless," described by Alfred North Whitehead in his brilliant chapter "The Century of Genius" in *Science and the Modern World*,[25] nature for Paley was a vibrant and live carnival of pleasurable activity where even swarms of shrimp on an ocean shore huddle "in a state of positive enjoyment." "What a sum, collectively, of gratification and pleasure have we here before our view!" he exclaimed in exultation (p. 319).

His second proposition—"that the Deity has added *pleasure* to animal sensations, beyond what was necessary for any other purpose" (p. 335)—was essentially a reinforcement of his first assertion; it claimed that besides providing living creatures with the means of existence, God also "superadded" the capacity for pleasure which, though not strictly necessary for life, rendered it more bearable. Thus, for example, although it is a requirement of survival to eat, it is not indispensable that food titillate the palate. "Why add pleasure to the act of eating," he asks rhetorically, "sweetness and relish to food? . . . Why should the juice of a peach, applied to the palate, affect the part so differently from what it does when rubbed upon the palm of the hand?" (p. 336). Other pleasures as well cannot be accounted for by any doctrine of necessity: the joys of sport and those "received from things, great, beautiful, or new" cannot be traced to survival; nor can the satisfaction of owning property—a pleasure which "communicates a charm to whatever is the object of it" (p. 341)—be accounted for if God were, as Hume claimed, a "rigid master." Only a benevolent God, a Deity of great goodness, would freely grant such happiness to all his creatures.

Yet, it was on this assertion that Paley's natural theology steered into shallow waters laden with one enormous danger; in a universe created by a benevolent and powerful deity, the origin of evil became an acute, embarrassing problem. Throughout the Enlightenment, theologians who no longer found solace in the powerful but unavoidably degrading myth of man's Fall, sought an alternate explanation which would account for man's perversity without vitiating his dignity. Some, like Soame Jenyns, simply denied the existence of evil; but the potent wisdom of Samuel Johnson seemed to reveal the bankruptcy of this myopic expedient.[26] Others, like Alexander Pope, admitted its existence but attempted to understand it by appealing to the elaborate metaphysical scheme known as the chain of being.[27] In general, however, the problem of theodicy—the oldest and most fundamental question of Christian thought—became the exposed flank of Enlightenment theology.

Though he openly admitted there was no "universal solution" to the problem (p. 342), Paley bravely endeavored to offer an answer consistent with his exuberant optimism. Yet, even his most compassionate sympathizers would probably grant that he failed; his reflections on the origin of evil contain some of the most jarring statements in the entire essay. After rejecting the "doctrine of general laws" and the chain of being as "too wide" and "difficult to apply" to particular circumstances, he resorted to the more "practical" claim that evil was only an aberration that was not without rewards and compensations. Thus, for example, physical pain "may be violent and frequent; but it is seldom both violent and long-continued: and its pauses and intermissions become positive pleasures. It has the power of shedding a satisfaction over intervals of ease, which . . . few enjoyments exceed" (p. 345). When Paley wrote this passage, he himself was suffering from the torturous pains of intestinal cancer; like Condorcet, he maintained his optimism even under the severest personal challenges. Nevertheless, this sanguine outlook—at one point he introduced a chart to prove that "few diseases are fatal"—must have been cold comfort to the less hearty souls who could not appreciate the "wonderful manner" in which mortal illness reconciles men to the idea of death (p. 346).

Yet, despite Paley's extensive and occasionally controversial discussion of God's attributes, it might be argued that his Deity remained a fleshless abstraction, a foreign and wholly unimaginable stranger for whom any feelings of love or fear would seem inappropriate. Neither omnipotence nor omniscience nor omnipresence is a quality which elicits concrete mental images; they were consciously intended not to. Whether or not this vagueness consequently meant that Paley's God was a transcendent deity—the distant "watchmaker" which many students seem to associate with the word "deism"—remains an open question. But a case can be made that the God portrayed in *Natural Theology* was as immediate and personal as those found in traditional religions, that he was within the realm of human comprehension and therefore of love.

This view partially turns on our interpretation of the initial analogy of proportionality which compared nature

to a watch, and God to a watchmaker. In interpreting such
an analogy, the major problem centers on whether Paley
has asserted the analogue univocally or equivocally. Both
approaches involve traps. If the terms within the analogy
were taken univocally—if the statements on either side of
the analogy stood in a legitimately proportional relation—then the theologian conceded an intimate kinship
between the watchmaker and God: the Deity became
deeply anthropomorphic. If, on the other hand, the analogy was asserted equivocally—if the wisdom involved in
constructing a watch was not entirely similar to that of
God creating nature—the result was a mystical and transcendent God of whom little accurate or precise knowledge could be posited.[28]

Enlightenment theologians never clearly resolved this
issue. On the one hand, by establishing final cause as the
essence of any phenomenon, they were in fact claiming
knowledge of an ultimate metaphysical truth and thereby
entering directly into the mind of God. Thus when Isaac
Barrow claimed in his sermon "The Being of God Proved
from the Frame of Human Nature" that there was "scarce
any attribute commonly ascribed to God, the existence
whereof we cannot show possible, yea very credible, by
shewing some degree . . . thereof discernible in man," he
was speaking in the language of a direct proportional
analogy.[29] In a similar manner, Robert Boyle once maintained in a sermon that although "full and adequate
knowledge" of the Deity was impossible, "we may not
only know very many things concerning Him, but, what is
more, may make an endless progress in that knowledge."[30]
Comparable illustrations could be multiplied in the works
of most natural theologians from Ray through Berkeley. In
an age when most Christian intellectuals associated a
knowledge of nature with the wisdom of God, it was no
coincidence that the mind of Newton was frequently
compared to that of the Deity.[31]

Yet, at some point in their discourse, most theologians restrained their intellectual pride and bowed to convention by disclaiming any authentic knowledge of God's ways. "We have ideas of his attributes, but what the real substance of anything is we know not," admitted Newton in the *Principia*. Others agreed. In a sermon, "Divine Predestination and Foreknowledge," delivered in 1709, William King argued that the true nature of the Deity lay beyond the realm of reason and logic, that God was "incomprehensible of human understanding." Peter Browne, whose *Procedure, Extent, and Limits of Human Understanding* exhaustively discussed the topic, argued at length that "we have no Idea of God, as he is in Himself; and it is for want of such an Idea, that we frame to ourselves the most excellent Conception of Him we can, by putting Together into one, the greatest Perfection we observe in the Creatures."[32]

Like Browne, Paley made clear that the attributes of God were convenient superlatives which were "beyond all comparison" and "greater than any which we experience in ourselves, than any which we observe in other visible agents" (pp. 308–9). Even granting this traditional qualification, however, the thrust of Paley's natural religion was toward a univocal application of analogy and a knowable rather than a transcendent God. Paley never denied that his analogy was proportional; he simply stated that God's power and wisdom were quantitatively greater than anything we had known.

> If we be careful to imitate the documents of our religion, by confining our explanations to what concerns ourselves, and do not affect more precision in our ideas than the subject allows of, the several terms which are employed to denote the attributes of the Deity may be made, even in natural religion, to bear a sense consistent with truth and reason, and not surpassing our comprehension. [P. 308]

The last phrases are crucial; they implied that through a careful study of the works of nature, men could come to know the "personality" of God in a direct and meaningful manner; that far from being a distant and transcendent Deity, God was as immediate and knowable as the human eye or the wing of a butterfly. "A man cannot lift his hand to his head," Paley wrote at one point, "without finding enough to convince him of the existence of a God" (p. 127).

This intimate familiarity which he felt for the Deity had already been manifested in such things as his praise of the epiglottis and his delight at the happiness of natural creatures. Like a litany, it recurred throughout the essay, attaining an emotional climax near the end of the book. To Paley, once the argument from design takes possession of the mind, "the world thenceforth becomes a temple, and life itself one continued act of adoration."

> The change is no less than this: that, whereas formerly God was seldom in our thoughts, we can now scarcely look upon anything without perceiving its relation to him. . . . So that the mind, as well as the eye, may either expatiate in variety and multitude, or fix itself down to the investigation of particular divisions of the science. And in either case it will rise up from its occupation, possessed by the subject, in a very different manner, and with a very different degree of influence, from what a mere assent to any verbal proposition which can be formed concerning the existence of the Deity. . . can produce upon the thoughts. . . . More especially may this difference be perceived, in the degree of admiration and of awe, with which the Divinity is regarded, when represented to the understanding by its own remarks, its own reflections, and its own reasoning, compared with what is excited by any language that can be used by others. The works of nature want only to be contemplated. [P. 375]

This declaration of faith again testifies to the profound, and often gravely misunderstood, inner spiritual life of the natural theologian. Rather than separate man from God by relegating him to the passive role of a distant watchmaker, the argument from design brought man *to* God, exciting in the observer passions greater than could be described "by any language . . . used by others." Reason —the gift of God—demanded that man should not accept Christianity merely on the basis of subjective feelings; that was enthusiasm. Instead, it required empirical proof for its assent to any religious proposition; but this proof, which was nature itself, reaffirmed that which was never really doubted and, more important, suddenly transformed the world into a vast spiritual sanctuary where every plant and animal awakened the deepest feelings of admiration and love.

Thus the primary purpose of natural religion—its function in the lives of the men who read it and who wrote it—was only tangentially related to its articulated goal of demonstrating the existence of a Deity. Paley never claimed that his cautious and generally sober lucubrations on the argument from design were intended to persuade the nonbeliever or convert the atheist; he was not a missionary. The overwhelming majority of his audience were already reliable Christians, and it was to their intellectual predilections and spiritual demands that he directed his message. "Occasions will arise to try the firmness of our most habitual opinions," he remarked, "and upon these occasions, it is a matter of incalculable use to feel our foundation; to find a support in argument for what we had taken upon authority" (p. 373). This was the first object of natural theology, its initial destination; the teleological argument assured the Enlightenment Christian that his religious faith was not founded solely on the treacherous sands of the human emotions. Religion was based on fact as well as feeling. As an arbiter of conduct and of belief, it could be justified before the stern tribunal of logic and science.

If natural theology expanded the dimensions of Christianity by encompassing within its fold the most recent discoveries of natural science, it also strengthened the spiritual bond between God and man which had always been the indispensable core of religious faith. Natural theology enunciated a prophecy as well as an apology. It predicted that the man who ventured forth into nature, searched its methods, and studied its secrets would undergo a spiritual transformation in which the world itself became a "temple" and life an "act of adoration." In everything he encountered he would feel the presence of God and discover that "One Being has been concerned in all" (p. 376). It was this profound inner change—an experience which the normally hardheaded Paley found difficult to define—that lay at the heart of natural theology.

Natural religion had one final effect. In its power to reaffirm and enlarge an existing faith in God, it led men back to revelation, the recorded testament of God's intervention in history. "The true theist will be the first to listen to *any* credible communication of Divine knowledge," Paley remarked at the conclusion of his *Natural Theology;* "his inward veneration of this great Being will incline him to attend with the utmost seriousness . . . all that is taught by a revelation, which gives reasonable proof of having proceeded from him" (p. 377). Revelation disclosed the particulars of religious belief; it provided the moral precepts which ought to govern actions among men. Yet, revelation itself could not be inviolate from the scrutiny of reason; it also should submit to the rigorous examination of objective analysis. To this end, Paley composed in the early 1790s two volumes of biblical criticism which, in exhaustive detail, sought to establish the historical credibility of the New Testament.

CHAPTER 4

Revealed Religion

THE ANALYSIS OF REVEALED RELIGION EMBODIED IN PALEY'S *Evidences of Christianity* and *Horae Paulinae* was constructed on the same assumptions and by the same methodology as his *Natural Theology*. Again, the argument was empirical, analogical, and dependent upon the laws of probability formulated by Isaac Newton and applied systematically to theology by Bishop Butler. Again, the assumption of causal uniformity—the critical link between Enlightenment science and religion—proved to be the unifying factor between nature and the revelations of the New Testament. And, as before, the deeper function of the discourse was only tangentially related to its avowed purpose. Paley's intensive study of the Bible thus became a major episode in the explanation of his unified and coherent vision of the world. Without the *Evidences*, his philosophy could easily be construed as deistic or even unitarian; without the *Natural Theology*, his biblical criticism would be robbed of the theoretical foundation of its central arguments.

The assumption of uniformity in nature, which buttressed the teleological argument for the existence of God, presupposed no limitations either of space or of time. The same laws of motion applied to ancient Greece as to modern Britain, and for this reason eighteenth-century theologians contended that the argument from design was

as apparent to the heathen philosophers of antiquity as it
was to modern thinkers. The implicit difficulty of Newton's third rule of reasoning, however, lay in the inescapable fact that Christianity originated in a single place
and at a specific point in history. The question thus became whether revelation, unlike natural religion, was
restricted only to certain peoples and, if so, why an omnipotent, omnipresent, and beneficent Creator would
limit the only path to salvation to a relatively primitive people in the eastern Mediterranean.

These awkward queries were raised most forcibly by
the deists. Matthew Tindal, John Toland, Anthony Collins, and others resolved to make Christianity genuinely
consistent with the premises of Newtonian science. This
meant banishing all the peculiarities that arose from the
religion's origin in a specific time and place, and substi-
tuting the more logical assertion that, as Toland entitled
his most famous book, Christianity was "as Old as the
Creation." This desire for rigourous consistency also implied that all recorded deviations from scientific law in the
New Testament could no longer be accepted on either
authority or naive faith. It was, therefore, Newton's third
rule that led, quite unexpectedly, to the protracted controversy over miracles.

In his *Discourse on the Miracles,* Thomas Woolston
argued that it was impossible to establish the value of
Christianity by invoking its own miracle stories; that such
accounts threw up "Absurdities, Impossibilities, and
Incredibilities" incompatible with the dignity of religion;
and that, consequently, the only avenue of escape from
these ancient illusions lay in the allegorical interpretation
of Scripture. The miracles thus became "an emblematical
Representation of the spiritual life" of Jesus, rather than
the systematic violation of immutable scientific law.[1]

This position prompted orthodox replies that determined the course of theological inquiry for a century to

come. To Woolston's first assertion, apologists such as Samuel Clarke fired back the counterargument that miracles were, in fact, "a sensible and compleat Demonstration of our Lord's Divine Commission" which allowed God to reveal his will to man. Moreover, miracles were not "absurd" departures from scientific law because, as Clarke put it, "There is no such thing as what Men commonly call the *Course of Nature* or the *Power of Nature.*"

> The Course of Nature, truly and properly speaking, is nothing else but the *Will of God* producing certain Effects in a continual, regular, constant and uniform Manner; which Course or Manner of Acting, being in every moment perfectly Arbitrary, is as easie to be altered at any time, as to be *preserved.*[2]

Finally, orthodox divines rejected the alternative of an allegorical exegesis of Scripture in favor of the more direct, literal interpretation. The Bible was "an authentic, genuine history," wrote Butler in his critically important *Analogy of Religion;* miracles could be made "to stand upon the same foot of historical evidence" as any other past event.[3]

The *Analogy* spelled doom for the deists not only because of its brilliant central thesis, but also because it launched orthodoxy on a new offensive. Henceforth, Christian divines could base their belief in revelation on a series of intricate, interdependent, and widely substantiated probabilities, immune to any single line of attack. In particular, the credibility of the Gospel came to be established on "a great variety of circumstantial evidence" whose compelling persuasiveness derived from its very diversity.[4] If no single piece of evidence "proved" the Christian religion, no individual slice of data disproved it either. It was the tactics of the courtroom applied to the mysteries of the cathedral.

Hume's arguments against miracles in his *Enquiry concerning Human Understanding* posed a new threat. After lodging the analytic objection that miracles violated laws of nature established by "firm and unalterable experience," he proceeded to challenge the empirical foundation of the orthodox position. No witnesses to a miracle story could be placed "beyond all suspicion of any design to deceive others," he began; and, adding a somewhat sophistical argument, he questioned whether the miracle of any single religion undercut the authority and reliability of all other religious miracles. In almost all cases, moreover, accounts of the miraculous took root "among ignorant and barbarous nations" whose people were easily carried away by the excesses of enthusiastic fervor. "Upon the whole," he concluded, "it appears that no testimony for any kind of miracle has ever amounted to a probability, much less to a proof."[5]

These arguments persuaded many contemporaries that Hume was a deist of the old school, and it was not until the posthumous publication of the *Dialogues* that the full strategy of his assault could be evaluated. Though most Christians chose to ignore his other writings, the attack on miracles attracted considerable attention. Pamphlets poured from the press, some offering balanced evaluations of his central argument, others only vituperative denunciations of the Scottish infidel.[6] Yet it was not until Paley published his *Evidences* in 1794 that orthodoxy found its definitive expression. In the eyes of most churchmen and Christian intellectuals, Paley rebutted Hume just as surely as Butler had routed the deists earlier in the century.

Paley's biblical analysis thus served two immediate purposes. First, it played a crucial role in his own informal system of philosophical theology. In his *Natural Theology*, he posed the most fundamental of all religious questions—does God exist? Now, in the *Evidences* and *Horae*

Paulinae, he asked whether that God had ever revealed himself in human history. As in his discussion of the teleological argument, his answer to this query took the form of a scientific treatise. The *Evidences* posited two major propositions that it substantiated with a complex analysis of the available evidence, including carefully reasoned responses to the more prominent objections lodged by skeptics. It pretended to assume nothing about its own arguments, hoping instead that its evidence would render its hypothesis as convincing as Newton's formulas.

Since Hume asked the same questions as Paley, it was necessary for Paley to dispose of Hume's alternate and antithetical answers. This constituted the second purpose of his biblical criticism; both the *Evidences* and *Horae Paulinae* were a unified and extensive refutation of Hume's essay on miracles. Paley mentioned Hume by name in the opening pages of the *Evidences* and constantly referred to his arguments and examples in the course of the book. This polemic against Hume—central to Paley's analysis of revealed religion—deserves further exploration.

II

Paley initiated his *Evidences* with a compressed analysis of Hume's most potent objection to miracles—that, as a violation of natural law, "the proof against a miracle, from the very nature of the fact, is as entire as any argument from experience can possibly be imagined."[7] With his characteristic penetration, the archdeacon recognized that this assertion stood "in the very threshold" of his own theory, acting as "a bar to every proof, and to all future reasoning upon the subject."[8] Once accept the absolute inviolability of scientific law, and the Resurrection, for example, becomes the wild delusion of a fanatic mind.

Paley thus accused Hume of a "want of argumentative justice" because his definition of miracles, while correct analytically, created an a priori case against their existence. In effect, Hume was asserting the fundamental reliability of the assumption of causal uniformity, claiming that no amount of human testimony could be of significant strength to overturn natural law. Such thinking was, at bottom, tautological, especially for a radical empiricist like Hume, and strongly implied a metaphysical bias that Paley wanted to flush out into the open. He sensed that Hume's objection stemmed from a preestablished view concerning the existence of a Deity itself; that is, that the rejection of miracles was founded on Hume's coexistent repudiation of the teleological argument. "As Mr. Hume has represented the question," he observed pointedly, "miracles are alike incredible to him who is previously assured of the constant agency of a Divine Being, and to him who believes that no such Being exists in the universe" (*E*, p. 7).

If, however, such rational proofs as the argument from design established beyond any reasonable doubt the existence of God, Hume's objection could be countered. For if God formulated the laws of nature, it was certainly within his power to violate these same laws to further his will on earth. "In a word," Paley wrote, "once believe that there is a God, and miracles are not incredible" (*E*, p. 7). The relationship between natural and revealed religion in Paley's philosophy was thereby neither coincidental nor forced; teleology formed a critical link in the interconnecting series of analogies and probabilities that sustained the system. Yet, in rebuffing Hume's definition, he was not dogmatically asserting his own in its place; unlike the rationalists, he was merely positing the notion that, a priori, neither view could be granted the seal of certainty.

The peculiarity of this situation merits notice. Hume, the philosopher whose *Treatise* and *Enquiry* brilliantly challenged the underlying assumption of the "new science," who robbed inductive reasoning of any claim to

perfect reliability and by his analysis of cause and effect
seriously undermined the premise of natural theology and
its purest expression, deism, was here asserting that same
"firm and unalterable" assumption of causal uniformity
as the decisive proof that miracles did not exist. As one of
his contemporaries aptly put it, Hume's claim that miracles were "contrary to experience" created "a distinction,
which not only the essay, but the whole tone of his philosophical writing shows evidently to have no meaning."9

This inconsistency did not escape Paley's attention. For
anyone to state absolutely that an occurrence was "contrary to experience," he observed, it would be necessary
for the individual himself to have been present to witness
whatever did take place. Otherwise the truth of the
statement could be substantiated only on the basis of
probability (*E*, p. 4). With classic ease, Paley had turned
the tables on his formidable adversary.

Paley's conceptual framework for the existence of miracles thus accorded well with those of Clarke and Butler.
Natural law was only part of God's law. As an Absolute
Being, God established an order in the Universe that was
only dimly comprehensible to his favored creatures. Part
of this order was the periodic revelation of his will—not, as
Hume contended, with a frequency that might jeopardize
scientific law, but only on extraordinary occasions.

> The force of experience as an objection to miracles, is
> founded in the presumption, either that the course of nature
> is invariable, or that, if it be ever varied, variations will be
> frequent and general. Has the necessity of this alternative
> been demonstrated? Permit us to call the course of nature the
> agency of an intelligent Being; and is there any good reason
> for judging this state of the case to be probable? Ought we
> not rather to expect that such a Being, on occasions of pecu-
> liar importance, may interrupt the order which he had ap-
> pointed, yet, that such occasions should return seldom; that
> these interruptions consequently should be confined to the

experience of a few; that the want of it, therefore, in many, should be matter neither of surprise nor objection? [*E*, p. 6]

Examples of this intervention permeate the New Testament. It was only through miracles that God could reveal his will to the disciples, thereby teaching man of a future state of existence.

Yet, in the formulation of his argument, Paley never assumed the existence of a Deity in order to establish the credibility of miracles. In contradistinction to Hume, his only point was "that in miracles adduced in support of revelation there is not any such antecedent improbability as no testimony can surmount" (*E*, p. 3). The battleground thus shifted from a dispute over logic to a specific discussion of evidence. Paley believed that if he could secure the trustworthiness of his empirical data, he would, ipso facto, establish the truth of Christian metaphysics. It was a large assumption and one not without grave flaws, but it underlines the ironic fact that in the miracle controversy it was Paley, and not Hume, who was more the authentic empiricist.

III

The empirical dispute revolved around part two of Hume's chapter on miracles where, in four objections, he attempted to demolish the credibility of the Christian witnesses. It was the first of these objections that most troubled Paley. The men who claimed to have seen the miraculous, Hume argued, could not be trusted because they lacked the proper education and "good sense" to distinguish fact from fantasy. More important, their integrity was questionable; they could not be considered "beyond all suspicion of any design to deceive others" and were probably frauds.[10]

Paley dedicated half the *Evidences* and all of *Horae Paulinae* to refuting this charge, and perhaps because it aroused his sincere moral indignation, his rebuttal elicited some of his best writing. Shrewd, lucid, incisive, he possessed an engaging capacity to identify himself with the early Christian disciples, to portray their problems in disseminating the message of Jesus, and to admire their persistence in the face of grueling hardship. Moreover, as a polemicist, he could defuse objections by anticipating and absorbing them into his own argument, thus conveying the impression of a man who had ruminated longer and deeper on the issues than his chosen adversary. This narrative and argumentative talent must not be underemphasized; in his thoroughness, balance, and precision, Paley ranked with the best apologists of the British Enlightenment.

He shaped his reply to Hume's first subsidiary objection in the form of a proposition: there is satisfactory evidence, he affirmed, that many "professing to be original witnesses of the Christian miracles, passed their lives in labours, dangers, and sufferings, voluntarily undergone in attestation of the accounts which they delivered, and . . . also submitted, from the same motives, to new rules of conduct" (*E*, p. 10). In other words, Paley refused to abide by Hume's standards of credibility; education, "good sense," and social standing were superficial criteria, indicating nothing of the inner man and the emotional mechanics of religious belief. Physical courage, personal dedication, and moral perseverence in pursuit of a cause—these were the outward manifestations of an authentic conviction and the trademarks of the early followers of Jesus. Constantly working in a hostile environment, these converts faced hatred, exile, martyrdom. In Paley's view, this was not the behavior of a fraud; in their suffering they proved their sincerity.

Paley established this argument cautiously. Whereas some apologists might deem it unnecessary to substantiate the claim that the early Christians suffered for their beliefs, he perceived in those actions the key to his argument. A vast diversity of evidence, he averred, testified to

the authenticity of their faith. First, the very nature of the
early church impeded its immediate acceptance and
forced the disciples to endure ostracism. The Jews expected the Messiah to be a king, not a carpenter; the
heathens were accustomed to a lax state religion, exclusive in its orientation and bound by ancient traditions
inimical to the new faith; Rome, "prejudice backed by
power" (*E*, p. 15), persecuted the early converts relent-
lessly. Ancient Roman sources themselves—the "conces-
sion of adversaries" (*E*, p. 24) since the authors were often
either indifferent to or unimpressed by Christians—
offered cogent testimony to the labors of the early disciples. Tacitus, Suetonius, the Younger Pliny, and others
had numerous accounts of Christians who preferred martyrdom to the renunciation of their faith; and these
reports were fully confirmed by the New Testament, the
central source of early Christian history.

Clearly, then, Christianity transformed men's lives utterly, changing fishermen into prophets and tax collectors
into preachers. "How new!" Paley suddenly interjected in
the midst of his analysis, "how alien from all their former
habits and ideas, and from those of every body about
them! What a revolution there must have been of opinions
and prejudices to bring the matter to this!" (*E*, p. 22).

This entire procedure—the cautious sifting of Roman
and Christian sources, the imaginative re-creation of the
social and intellectual hostility that could have smashed
the young religion on the rocks of hatred and indifference,
the genuine awe Paley felt for the courage and dedication
of the early apostles—turns, however, on one critical assumption concerning the dynamics of the conversion experience. As an eighteenth-century Christian empiricist,
weaned on the logic and epistemology of John Locke,
Paley sincerely believed it was the miracles, and not the
message of Jesus, that drove men to the extremes of
endurance.

A Galilean peasant was announced to the world as a divine law-giver. . . . This . . . was too absurd a claim to be either imagined, or attempted, or credited. In whatever degree, or in whatever part, the religion was *argumentative*, when it came to the question, "Is the carpenter's son of Nazareth the person whom we are to receive and obey?" there was nothing but the miracles attributed to him, by which his pretensions could be maintained for a moment. . . . Miraculous evidence lay at the bottom of the argument. In the *primary* question, miraculous pretensions, and miraculous pretensions alone, were what they had to rely upon. [*E*, pp. 61, 63]

The thrust of Paley's first proposition centered on the simple belief that men do not die for a lie; but underneath this noble assertion lay the more dubious proposition that, not unlike eighteenth-century Latitudinarians, the early disciples demanded and got reasonable evidence—visible signs perceived by the senses—that solidified their faith in the new master and fueled their religious zeal. Though it is easy to condemn this obvious anachronism in Paley's writing—Leslie Stephen makes sport of it in his *History of English Thought*[11]—this same assumption lurked behind Hume's charge that the apostles may have been frauds. To both Hume and Paley, miracles were either literally true or literally false.

One alternative explanation for miracles remained unanswered by Paley. Having demonstrated to his satisfaction that the early Christians passed their lives in danger and suffering "solely in consequence of their belief" in miracles, he next confronted the possibility that the original story of Jesus' life, including the performance of miracles, may have been fabricated by later copyists and historians. This was not a far-fetched anxiety; much of ancient history remained shrouded behind the contradictory renditions of later chroniclers, and as a seasoned Christian apologist fully aware of the weapons in his arsenal, Paley was loath to pass up an opportunity to parade his best material. "There is not a document," he began, "or a scrap of account, either contemporary with the commencement of Christianity, or extant within many ages after that commencement, which assigns a history substantially different from ours" (*E*, pp. 64–65).

The transmission of the Gospels was a topic that excited biblical scholars in the eighteenth century, and it was from this tradition of research that Paley borrowed heavily in composing the longest single chapter in the *Evidences*, "Of the Authenticity of the Historical Scriptures." Here he recapitulated the most important discoveries of his scholarly predecessors—that, for example, "the Scriptures were in very early times collected into a distinct volume" (*E*, p. 139); that they "were publicly read and expounded in religious assemblies" (*E*, p. 141); that "Commentaries were anciently written upon the Scriptures" (*E*, p. 144). If today the predominant element in this analysis seems to be its literal-mindedness, for Paley it removed the remaining obstacle in his quest to establish the credibility of the early converts. From these pages of ingenious synthesis emerged the overwhelming conclusion that the present Gospels "actually proceeded from the authors whose names they bear" (*E*, p. 179).

It seems a modest assertion, but it was a significant link in the chain of probabilities that Paley flung against Hume, and it employed a method of biblical exegesis that dated back to the Reformation. When Calvin repudiated the authoritative and allegorical interpretation of Scripture prominent in the Middle Ages, he imposed a heavy burden on the Protestant rationalists of the seventeenth and eighteenth centuries. Both the discoveries of the scientific revolution and the arguments of natural religion dictated to Enlightenment Christians that the Bible ought to possess those qualities of simplicity, order, and consistency which God had clearly revealed in his vast creation. It thus became incumbent upon biblical scholars to turn a blind eye on those elements of Scripture which were all too human—and fallible—stressing instead those aspects of harmony and sweet reasonableness which best accorded with their scientific bias.[12]

The result was an artful attempt in the early eighteenth century "to represent the Doctrine of our Saviour in its Original Simplicity" and, as Clarke put it, to discover "the most natural meaning of the Text." This impulse lay behind Locke's *Reasonableness of Christianity* and his lesser-known but influential *Paraphrase . . . on the Epistles of St. Paul.* "One may see his thoughts were all of a piece in all of his Epistles," Locke wrote in reference to Paul; "his notions were at all times uniform, and consistently the same, though his expressions were various."[13]

This gradual process of rationalizing the sacred texts of Christianity suffered a rude jolt from the deists, however, when in what the orthodox insisted was an unforgivable perversion of their original intention, they applied the criteria of uniformity to the very existence of miracles themselves; that is, when they extended scientific reasoning to the events of the New Testament rather than simply to the written record of those events. As in the case of Woolston, this approach left no alternative but a return to an allegorical interpretation of the New Testament, if Scripture was to retain any meaning at all. To the orthodox, the deists thus represented a reactionary tendency in biblical criticism, since an acceptance of their major arguments signaled a return to the discredited analytic methods of the Middle Ages.

The threat of pure deism thereby handed scholarly biblical critics a new task, not entirely uncongenial to their old pursuits. Whereas previously they had sought a uniform pattern among the conflicting statements of the Gospels in order to make revelation consistent with the assumptions of science and natural religion, their purpose now was to establish the very credibility of the events

which the various texts described. This called for a shift
in tactics. Greater attention was paid to the similarity
between secular and religious descriptions of the early
Christian church, and the question of the Bible's transmission through history suddenly became much more
important. Yet, in their essential method of exegesis, the
biblical critics retained their original premise that—as
in science—harmony, simplicity, and order were the best
indications of truth.

The most famous of these scholars was Nathaniel Lardner, the congenitally deaf Nonconformist who devoted
thirty-three years to compiling his *Credibility of the Gospel History.* An encyclopedia of esoteric details, Lardner's
volumes were grounded on the hope that "if the gospel-
history be credible, the truth of the Christian religion
cannot be contested."

> The evidence of the truth of any history is either internal or
> external. The internal evidence depends on the probability of
> the things related, the consistence of the several parts, and
> the plainness and simplicity of the narration. The external
> evidence consists of the concurrence of other ancient writers
> of good credit, who lived at, or near the time, and who bear
> testimony to the books themselves, and their authors, or the
> facts contained in them.[14]

In seventeen volumes of crushing detail, Lardner drove
home his major theme. Scrupulous to the point of ped-
antry in his citations and compulsively thorough, he covered the ancient sources from St. Matthew to Annobius,
omitting nothing that might be relevant. It was from this
rich quarry that Paley extracted many of the historical
details for his protracted discussion of the Bible's credibility in his works on revealed religion, more than once
freely acknowledging his debt to the "excellent" Lardner,
"who never overstates a point of evidence" (*HP*, p. 254).

The *Evidences* thus merged two traditions of orthodoxy
in the eighteenth century, both born of the deist chal-

lenge. The one, theoretical and argumentative, sustained itself on a complicated series of interconnecting analogies between natural and revealed religion, and was almost the exclusive property of Bishop Butler. It was this style of argument that Paley invoked in his opening discussion of Hume's essay. The other tradition, empirical and cumulative, relied heavily on the scrutiny of ancient sources and was best realized in the massive tomes of Nathaniel Lardner. The seminal assumption here was that consistency disproved fraud, and harmony established truth. Since the disciples witnessed miracles and recorded their experiences, the validity of Christianity turned on the authenticity of those written testaments. Thus, the same standards of harmony and uniformity that led skeptics to dispute the miraculous convinced the orthodox of its existence.

It was at this stage in the argument that Paley made his unique contribution to eighteenth-century apologetics. *Horae Paulinae* antedated the *Evidences* by four years, but thematically it was the offspring, not the progenitor, of the later book.[15] Like the first proposition of the *Evidences*, it concerned itself with the problem of fraud and thus refuted one of Hume's adamant protests against Christian miracles.

The New Testament contains a history of St. Paul—the Acts of the Apostles—and also thirteen letters believed to have originated from his pen. Paley pretended to assume the authenticity of neither; "the reader is at liberty to suppose these writings to have been lately discovered in the library of the Escurial, and to come to our hands destitute of any extrinsic or collateral evidence whatever" (*HP*, p. 5).

Now agreement between a man's history and his letters did not establish the credibility of either: if the letters were genuine, a history could easily be fabricated from the narrative evidence contained within them. Conversely, the letters could have been forged from the history. Final-

ly, both history and letters could have been compiled from
floating reports and traditions. In all cases, however, the
conformity "must be the effect of design."

> In examining, therefore, the agreement between ancient
> writings, the character of truth and originality is unde-
> signedness: and this test applies to every supposition; for,
> whether we suppose the history to be true, but the letters
> spurious; or, the letters to be genuine, but the history false;
> or, lastly, falsehood to belong to both . . . the same inference
> will result—that either there will be no agreement between
> them, or the agreement will be the effect of design. [*HP*,
> pp. 8–9]

Broad and explicit agreements between the letters and
Acts proved little, since "such is the ordinary expedient
of every forgery"; instead, the more "minute, circuitous,
or oblique" the illustrations, the stronger the case (*HP*,
p. 10).

Paley devoted the remainder of his remarkable study to
scores of specific "undesigned coincidences" to prove his
point. Thus, for example,

> . . . when I read in the Acts of the Apostles, that when "Paul
> came to Derbe and Lystra, behold a certain disciple was
> there, named Timotheus, the son of a certain woman *which
> was a Jewess;*" and when, in an epistle addressed to Timothy,
> I find him reminded of his "having known the Holy Scriptures
> *from a child,*" which implies that he must, on one side or
> both, have been brought up by Jewish parents: I conceive
> that I remark a coincidence which shows, by its very *obliq-
> uity,* that scheme was not employed in its formation. [*HP*,
> p. 11]

Paley admitted that not all of his examples were equally
persuasive, but he insisted that his general argument did
not suffer because of this. As in his *Natural Theology,* he

was building a probability argument in which no single piece of evidence either clinched or demolished his central theme.

Horae Paulinae was one of Paley's shrewdest productions, combining a clever and original thesis with a subtle analysis of the biblical text. The book exploded the theory, often articulated in the nineteenth century, that he was merely a popularizer, intellectually incapable of thinking through a new idea. In its Cartesian refusal to assume anything essential and its painstaking dissection of the New Testament, *Horae Paulinae* anticipated the analytic methods of the Broad Church movement of the nineteenth century—the attempt to read the Bible "like any other book"—and the New Criticism of the twentieth. More important, it added another file of empirical evidence to the cavalcade of probabilities deployed against Hume.

Hume had written that "a wise man . . . proportions his belief to the evidence," that "all probability . . . supposes an opposition of experiments and observations, where the one side is found to overbalance the other, and to produce a degree of evidence, proportioned to the superiority." Yet, to his objection that the corroboration of miracles demanded men "beyond any suspicion of any design to deceive others,"[16] it was Paley who produced the most substantiating evidence. Sifting testimony culled from ancient sources, he argued that the early converts demonstrated their sincerity by their suffering; that they lived and died for the miracles they had witnessed. Moreover, their testimony was neither forged, lost, nor altered during its transmission through the centuries. Borrowing Hume's suggestion, he had constructed a probability argument founded upon a blueprint of self-imposed rules and buttressed with a diversity of sources sufficient, he hoped, to persuade the "wise man."

IV

Hume added muscle to his argument by pointing to the abundance of miracles in other religions which, like Christianity, claimed a monopoly of truth. Hinduism, Buddhism, Islam, and the followers of Jesus all posited mutually exclusive cosmologies that justified themselves by stories of supernatural intervention. "Every miracle, therefore, pretended to have been wrought in any of these religions, . . . as its direct scope is to establish the particular system to which it is attributed; so has it the same force, though more indirectly, to overthrow every other system."[17] Since religious miracles cannot all be equally true, Hume's logic ran, all must be equally false.

This argument was not unique to Hume. The deists had pursued it vigorously earlier in the century; and it had spawned a sizable literary rebuttal from orthodox churchmen who, in their eagerness to reduce confusion, often succeeded only in accenting the contradictions of their own position. The usual tactic was to throw up a defensive wall around the early Christian miracles and, from this guarded perimeter, launch attacks on the surrounding competitors.[18] It would be this strategy, with all its ingenious distinctions but unavoidable inconsistencies, that Paley would adopt.

He confronted the problem with characteristic directness. "There is NOT satisfactory evidence," he stated, "that persons pretending to be original witnesses of any other similar miracles, have acted in the same manner" as the early Christian converts (*E*, p. 182). Paley was a utilitarian and consequently a man of deeds, not motives. Unlike the apostles, witnesses of other alleged miracles did not undergo the trials, suffering, and dangers that would have lent credibility to their tales. Prolonged ordeal was, once again, the criterion of truth.

He followed up this line of reasoning with a series of distinctions that separated in his own mind the Christian accounts from their later imitations. In effect, this meant that several "proofs" of later miracles could be conveniently discounted. Some were reported only years after the event occurred; others sprang from "transient rumors" (*E*, p. 186); still others required nothing more than an "otiose assent," since they were "stories upon which nothing depends, in which no interest is resolved, nothing is to be done or changed in consequence of believing them" (*E*, p. 190). Finally, as in the case of Catholic miracles, some merely affirmed established opinions, demanding no sacrifice or inner transformation of the witness. "It has long been observed," he said wryly, "that Popish miracles happen in Popish countries; that they make no converts" (*F*, p. 191).

As for the later miracles themselves, several alternate explanations accounted for their origin. Some were simply false perceptions, the delusions of a credulous mind. Others, as in the prophecies of the ancient Greek oracles, were only occasionally successful "whilst failures [were] forgotten, or suppressed." Still others remain "doubtful," no matter what the claims, and, finally, there were "accounts, in which the variation of a small circumstance may have transformed some extraordinary appearance, or some critical coincidence of events, into a miracle; stories, in a word, which may be resolved into exaggeration" (*E*, pp. 199–201).

Into these categories Paley relegated Hume's three specific illustrations of palpably false miracles, explaining their incidence in rationalistic terms. Unlike Hume, he did not believe that to discredit any miracle story necessarily shed doubt on the intrinsic merit of all others. Each demanded individual scrutiny, and most no doubt were false. As he had emphasized at the outset, if a miracle were repeated frequently throughout history, it would "cease to be a miracle . . . and would totally destroy the use and purpose for which it was wrought" (*E*, p. 6).

Paley was nevertheless, like the apologist Conyers Middleton, on precarious ground which threatened to collapse if ever he turned his own arguments back upon his earlier proposition. The whole debate was fraught with paradoxes—Hume invoking what in other contexts he regarded as the uncertain notion of causal uniformity to dispute the existence of miracles, Paley using Hume's own later arguments to demolish all accounts other than those in the New Testament. These intellectual gyrations indicated a subterranean current of emotion about the acknowledged issues that, as in the debate over teleology, was rarely visible but always shaped the terrain of the argument. For Paley, this current finally erupted on the surface when Hume lodged his most significant and prophetic objections to the empirical foundation of miracle stories.

V

"A religionist may be an enthusiast, and imagine he sees what has no reality," Hume suggested in his second subsidiary objection to miracles; and he continued this line of attack in his third point: "It forms a strong presumption against all supernatural and miraculous relations, that they are observed chiefly to abound among ignorant and barbarous nations . . . [where] men's inclination to the marvelous has full opportunity to display itself."[19] For Hume, unlike the deists, it was not enough simply to repudiate miracles; it was also crucial to explain what in human nature encouraged their creation and sustained their transmission through history. His answer to these queries pointed to the same fundamental impulse that led men to fabricate a God in the first place, an impulse he had explored brilliantly in his *Natural History of Religion* and further elaborated in the *Dialogues*. Ultimately, all of Hume's religious writings were various threads of the same fabric, designed to protect and thereby liberate men from their persistent tendency to project themselves upon the unfathomable operations of the universe.

One essential difference between Hume and Paley turned on an assumption which was elucidated early in the *Evidences*.

> The existence of the testimony is a phaenomenon; the truth of the fact solves the phaenomenon. If we reject this solution, we ought to have some other to rest in; and none, even by our adversaries, can be admitted, which is not inconsistent with the principles that regulate human affairs and human conduct at present, or which makes men *then* to have been a different kind of being from what they are now. [*E*, p. 8]

The last phrase was crucial. Paley believed that, in their basic assumptions and fundamental rationality, the early followers of Jesus were not unlike natural theologians of the eighteenth century and that, consequently, extraordinary occurrences such as miracles provided these disciples with convincing proofs of Christ's divinity. Unlike Hume, Paley contended that the miracles of Jesus were witnessed by reasonable men in full possession of their mental faculties.

This assumption that men in ancient times were not "different kind of beings from what they are now" also underlay Paley's analysis of the character of Jesus. In brief, he portrayed Christ as a utilitarian of the Enlightenment variety. "Our Lord enjoined no austerities," he wrote in his chapter "Of the Morality of the Gospels"; "he not only enjoined none as absolute duties, but he recommended none as carrying men to a higher degree of Divine favour" (*E*, p. 247). Above all, Christ was not an enthusiast; "this spirit," Paley asserted indignantly, "certainly did not

dictate our Saviour's conduct, either in his treatment of
the religion of his country, or in the formation of his own
institution. In both he displayed the soundness and mod-
eration of his judgement" (*E*, p. 249). Moreover, what
was true of Jesus applied with equal force to St. Paul. As
Paley once described it, Paul's moral code was "every
where calm, pure, and rational" (*HP*, p. 270).

Thus, if Hume claimed that miracles sprang from an age
that fostered the endless fantasies of the religious enthusiast, Paley countered with the notion that both Jesus and
Paul were as "well-instructed, cool and judicious" as any
Enlightenment philosopher (*E*, p. 249). As before, Paley
gathered inspiration for this view from the assumption of
uniformity, which erected no barriers of space and time.
Thus, even though both the *Evidences* and *Horae Paulinae*
were based on a painstaking examination of ancient
sources, both were radically unhistorical.

Yet, Hume's position was no less so. Despite his reputation as a historian and his implicit suggestion that miracles could be wrought only in a unique historical milieu,
his inquiry into the supernatural was as much a projection
of his normative values as that of the archdeacon. Where
they differed was not in their view of history, but in their
estimate of the religious man. Like Paley, Hume believed
"men *then*" to be like those of his own times, but to him
that implied they were superstitious, credulous, and prone
to anthropomorphism, even when they professed to be,
like Cleanthes in the *Dialogues*, rational in their theology.
In Hume's view of the world, the truly enlightened comprised a small elite indeed.

To Paley, Hume suffered from the same perceptual
deficiency that plagued Edward Gibbon; in their desire to
remain aloof from the feelings, pleasures, and daily strug-
gles of the mass of men, both were fundamentally incapable of understanding the mysteries and joys of deep
religious experience. As Paley put it in another context,

contempt, prior to examination, is an intellectual vice, from which the greatest faculties of mind are not free. I know not, indeed, whether men of the greatest faculties of mind are not the most subject to it. Such men feel themselves seated upon an eminence. Looking down from their height upon the follies of mankind, they behold contending tenets wasting their idle strength upon one another, with the common disdain of the absurdity of them all. This habit of thought . . . is extremely dangerous; and more apt, than almost any other disposition, to produce hasty and contemptuous, and, by consequence, erroneous judgements, both of persons and opinions. [*E,* p. 396]

"How do you refute a *sneer?*" Paley once remarked when asked his opinion of Gibbon's *Decline and Fall of the Roman Empire.*[20] Like Hume, Gibbon had composed more of a polemic against Christianity than a detached analysis of its authenticity and historical importance. To Gibbon, the transplanted Roman, Christianity was a fanatic sect that refused to abide by the reasonable and tolerant injunctions of the Roman imperium. He refused to look into the inner life of the religion, its aspirations and comforts, and thereby misunderstood it.

Paley never praised enthusiasm, but he knew that the essence of Christianity was nevertheless internal and mysterious. As he put it in the *Evidences:*

The kingdom of heaven is within us. That which is the substance of the religion, its hopes and consolation, its intermixture with the thoughts by day and by night, the devotion of the heart, the control of appetite, the steady direction of the will to the commands of God, is necessarily invisible. Yet upon these depend the virtue and the happiness of millions. [*E,* p. 417]

Thus, like his *Natural Theology,* both the *Evidences* and *Horae Paulinae* were the external manifestations of an inward faith which, as he often acknowledged, were never intended to convert the unbeliever or to change the mind of the convinced skeptic. "The inspiration of the historical Scriptures," he wrote in the conclusion to his *Evidences*, "the nature, degree, and extent of that inspiration, are questions undoubtedly of serious discussion; but they are questions amongst Christians themselves, and not between them and others" (*E*, p. 432). Where Hume and Paley ultimately differed, of course, was not simply in their estimate of the religious man, but in their religiosity itself. And that, Paley believed, could not be changed by rational dialogue.

If Paley suggested that revealed religion was, as it always had been, a fundamentally personal encounter with God, of closer kinship to poetry than to abstract science, he rarely emphasized this aspect of his thought. This encounter was an implicit understanding with his Christian readers rather than an outright proclamation; it was not his purpose to appeal to the heart. For this reason, he exposed himself to the criticism of the English Romantics, who dismissed his analysis as sterile, tedious, and void of spiritual content. Yet, to the extent that his biblical studies were an extended reply to Hume, there was no other alternative. The Scottish philosopher had laid down the challenge and chosen the weapons. As an apologist confident of his arguments and evidence, Paley was an obliging opponent equal, his contemporaries believed, to the task.

CHAPTER 5

Ethical and Political Thought

PALEY'S ETHICS AND POLITICS, LIKE HIS BIBLICAL criticism, were intimately related to his natural theology. The logical problems and underlying assumptions of the teleological argument for the existence of God provided a conceptual framework, a blueprint for analysis, which Paley applied with systematic thoroughness when he confronted the difficult task of building a system of ethics. The link between morals and theology, like that between natural and revealed religion, lay in a series of interconnecting analogies; it was from his observations of *telos* in natural phenomena—the adaptation of means to ends for beneficent purposes—that he derived his notion of utility and the conviction that God willed human happiness. A critical portion of the *Principles* was thus tied to the mathematical method of reasoning; it was abstract, deductive, and shared with rationalism the belief in the "fitness of Nature."

Yet, if Paley's morals retained features of the mathematical turn of mind he had acquired as a Cambridge undergraduate, in the *Principles* he also attempted openly to escape the pitfalls of abstract reasoning. "The reader becomes impatient when he is detained by disquisitions which have no other object than the settling of terms and phrases," he wrote in the preface; and consequently the works of previous ethicists were "not sufficiently adapted to real life and to actual situations." For his own part, he

would compose a work that would "accommodate both
the choice of the subjects and the manner of handling
them to the situations which arise in the life of an inhabi-
tant of this country in these times."[1]

Thus, Paley was both a practical and, at bottom, a
provincial moralist whose preoccupation with the immediate and concrete dwarfed his concern for the theoretical
issues which had engrossed his predecessors. Much of the
Principles concentrated on problems which other ethicists
were likely to regard, scornfully, as pedestrian and ba-
nal—the mutual responsibilities of labor contracts, for example, and the duties of parents to their children. Through
the maze of these mundane perplexities, Paley offered a
thread of escape. His work was a technical guidebook, a
kind of moral Baedeker, to the ethical concerns of the
young, propertied Englishmen he encountered as a teacher, and it endured as a Cambridge text precisely because
it confronted the minor but nevertheless critical moral
issues other philosophers ignored.

It would be unfruitful, therefore, to dwell upon or condemn Paley's occasional philosophic inconsistencies; he
was a pragmatic moralist writing for a practical age. In the
interplay between abstract theoretical principles and
immediate realities, he inevitably chose the latter, the "is"
over the "what might be." Unlike Bentham, he rarely led
his readers into uncharted waters, preferring instead to
demonstrate how existing institutions and practices already suited the basic injunctions of morals and politics.
This conservative thrust was partially the result of the kind
of thinking implicit in natural theology, where existing
means were shown to fit given ends, but it was also em-
bedded in the North Country personality of the author.
Paley was, above all, a man of common sense who, like
Samuel Johnson, instinctively distrusted the innovative
and the untested. In this mistrust, he reflected far more
accurately than Bentham the aspirations and prejudices of
his age.

The *Principles* was thus important for two reasons. First, it was a pivotal component in Paley's system of philosophy, a system that logically began with a proof of God's existence and from it evolved a theodicy, a method of biblical criticism, and a standard of moral behavior. The *Principles* informed men of their duty to the God described in the *Natural Theology*. Second, in both its abstract principles and its specific recommendations, it was a kind of barometer for the intellectual climate of late eighteenth-century England. The fundamental tenets of theological utilitarianism were deeply ingrained in the moral thought of the Enlightenment, and as a textbook writer who was "more than a mere compiler" (p. xv), Paley distilled and crystallized the best arguments of his distinguished predecessors into a single, coherent doctrine that for generations of university students would come to represent the ethical stance of the preceding era. Discounting its few controversial passages, the *Principles* reflected the ethical orthodoxy of a large and powerful group of eighteenth-century Englishmen who, though often not articulate themselves, found a lucid spokesman in the archdeacon.

Like the best textbooks, the *Principles* was well organized. It began with a series of "Preliminary Considerations" that embodied the central postulates of the work, then proceeded to a lengthy discussion of men's rights and duties that resulted from these principles, and concluded with an often brilliant survey of the "Elements of Political Knowledge." Since Paley was a master at constructing an argument, there seems little reason for the present analysis to deviate from the broad outlines of his general organization.

II

In both his theory of value and of obligation, Paley was a eudemonist who, like ethicists from Aristotle onward, believed that the good lay in human happiness. He defined the term as that condition when "the amount or aggregate of pleasure exceeds that of pain" (p. 15) and thereby placed himself in line with the conventional wisdom of eighteenth-century utilitarianism. Like most Enlightenment moralists, he grounded his analysis on the prescient insight that most ethical statements reflected the emotional and intellectual proclivities of the moral agent, rather than some vaguely defined moral absolute. Lockean epistemology taught that man's most basic instinct was to seek pleasure and avoid pain, and thus Paley, eschewing more ethereal and altruistic standards of value, derived his notion of the good from the hedonists.

Paley believed that pleasures differed only in "continuance and intensity" (p. 16) but, anticipating John Stuart Mill, dissociated himself from the popular notion of vulgar hedonism. There were solid utilitarian reasons why happiness did not consist in sensual pleasures; they continued "but a little while at a time" (p. 16), were spoiled by repetition, and blunted the appetite for higher things. Nor was happiness an exemption from care or labor, since "a moderate pain, upon which the attention may fasten and spend itself is to many a refreshment: as a fit of the gout will sometimes cure the spleen" (p. 19). Finally, happiness had nothing in common with high position or the accumulation of wealth. These were false mental associations that failed to take into account that it was the striving for a goal, rather than its attainment, which offered comfort and satisfaction.

Though most eighteenth-century moralists invoked happiness as a standard in their ethical treatises, few took time to delineate it precisely, and it remained one of the century's looser terms. Paley was more exact in his meaning and with customary thoroughness presented a four-part definition. First, felicity involved the ideal of human benevolence. Like Milton before him, Paley could not respect a cloistered virtue; morality had to be tested on an open stage and not simply rehearsed behind the scenes. Second, happiness meant pursuing a significant goal in life and dedicating all one's energies and faculties to it. Because he detested the "intolerable vacuity of mind" (p. 23) which characterized men of leisure, he argued that men needed something to work toward, something meaningful around which to plan their lives. This involved the third ingredient in his recipe for happiness: "the prudent constitution of the habits." Having arrived at a goal, men should carefully regulate their daily schedules for a variety of enjoyments; "the advantage is with those habits which allow of an indulgence in the deviation from them" (p. 25). To appreciate the value of multiple interests, however, an individual had to be in good health; and this ancient standard he deemed the fourth and final element in his formula for personal happiness.

Initially, the most striking feature of this prescription for the felicitous life seems to be its utter banality. Yet, cloaked behind the obvious lay an assumption crucial to the archdeacon's moral thought. In his four-part definition, the cardinal tenet was his emphasis on what he called "engagement"; it was the foundation of his other reflections on happiness; it recurred frequently throughout his writings and it was always stressed with greatest vigor:

The great principle of human satisfaction is *engagement*.

Now wherein . . . consists the satisfaction of any life whatever? They who have observed human nature most closely will tell you, with one voice, that it consists in a succession of exercise and rest, in the exertion of our faculties in some pursuit which interests them, and in the repose of these faculties after such exertion.[2]

Whatever be the fate or reception of this work [*Principles*] it owes its author nothing. In sickness and in health, I have found in it that which can alone alleviate the one, or give enjoyment to the other,—occupation and engagement. [P. xx]

Happiness consisted in living by a standard which was self-imposed and self-realized. It was self-imposed because the choice of activity·remained radically individual; each man was responsible for choosing his own "pleasurable engagements."

> This requires two things: judgment in the choice of *ends* adapted to our opportunities; and a command of imagination, so as to be able, when the judgment had made its choice of an end, to transfer the pleasure to the *means:* after which, the end may be forgotten as soon as we will. [P. 24]

Unlike the phenomena of nature, which were created by God with a specific purpose, each man was responsible for selecting his own purpose in life, his final cause. Yet, as in nature where God adapted the various mechanisms of the eye for the purpose of seeing, each man must adapt himself—his talents and his limitations—for the accomplishment of his chosen end.

Christianity, through its promise of an after-life, offered an incentive to meaningful engagement matched by no other activity. The Christian "has constantly before his eyes an object of supreme importance . . . and of which the pursuit (which can be said of no pursuit besides) lasts him to his life's end" (p. 24). Moreover, the eternal bliss guaranteed to the faithful provided him with the best hope of continuing and intensifying pleasure, albeit of the ethereal variety. The notion of Christian engagement thereby dovetailed conveniently into Paley's general theory of value.

Paley defined moral virtue as "the doing good to mankind, in obedience to the will of God, and for the sake of everlasting happiness" (p. 28). In a single stroke, he thus encompassed the subject ("the good of mankind"), rule ("the will of God"), and motive ("everlasting happiness") of the moral life. To Paley, the undeniable demands of self-interest coincided, rather than conflicted, with the needs of society: one unselfishly contributed to the common good for the selfish purpose of achieving the pleasures of heaven and avoiding the pains of hell. Paley thus tried to persuade his readers to become utilitarian for the same, somewhat unflattering reason he thought they had become Christian—"for the sake of everlasting happiness." For this reason, he has been called a theological utilitarian.[3]

Although Paley admitted that his belief in a future life, "the foundation upon which the whole fabric rests" (p. 43), was strictly an article of faith, it provided his ethics with a moral sanction that still exerted a powerful grip over many of his readers. He was convinced that he had bridged the gap between self-interest and social interest, thereby solving one of the central predicaments of Enlightenment theory. Secular utilitarians, such as Bentham and Hume, would dismiss this Christian motive for moral behavior as ethically reprehensible and metaphysically false, but would find the task of reconstructing ethics without the traditional sanctions difficult to execute.

Yet, by resolving one problem, Paley created another. His definition of moral virtue not only combined a prescription for utilitarian moral behavior with a conventional religious sanction, it also asserted that this ethic was "the will of God." It was precisely at this point that Paley's *Principles of Moral and Political Philosophy* meshed logically with his *Natural Theology* and his *Evidences of Christianity,* molding them into a coherent system of thought.

To Paley, as to many thinkers before him, God's will could be found either in Scripture or in nature, either in revealed or in natural religion. "The method of coming at the will of God concerning any action by the light of nature," he asserted, "is to inquire into 'the tendency of the action to promote or diminish the general happiness.' "

This rule proceeds upon the presumption, that God Almighty wills and wishes the happiness of his creatures; and, consequently, that those actions, which promote that will and wish, must be agreeable to him; and the contrary. . . . This presumption is the foundation of our whole system. [P. 45]

The empirical proof of this critical assertion was elaborated in his brief chapter "The Divine Benevolence," where he outlined what eventually became the *Natural Theology.*

No anatomist ever discovered a system of organization calculated to produce pain and disease; or in explaining the parts of the human body, ever said, This is to irritate; this is to inflame; this duct is to convey the gravel to the kidneys; this gland to secrete the humour which forms the gout: if by chance he come at a part which he knows not the use, the most he can say is, that it is useless: no one ever suspects that it is put there to incommode, to annoy, or to torment. [P. 47]

Since the purpose of each contrivance, its final cause, was not to harm a creature and since God created all things, it followed that the Deity was benevolent. The argument's major premise was based on a negative; that is, Paley demonstrated that evil was not the purpose of the contrivance. But behind the negative lay a positive assertion which constituted the thrust of the discussion; the adaptation of means to ends in all natural phenomena served a useful purpose. It promoted the happiness of the creature.

By analogy, Paley concluded that it was the "utility of any moral rule alone, which constituted the obligation of it," and he compressed this moral rule into a simple epigram, "Whatever is expedient, is right" (pp. 48–49). Thus, although "everlasting happiness" remained the motive for ethical behavior, it was "expediency"—a rule derived from God's will revealed in nature—that determined moral rectitude. Unfortunately, however, the term "expediency" would be gravely misunderstood, even by his sympathetic readers. Thus, for example, the negative connotations of the word repelled the Harvard moralists of the early ninetecnth century, who reversed the rule to read "Whatever is right, is expedient."⁴ True, "expediency" could mean "useful" or "politic" as opposed to "just" or "right," but Paley included in his work an extensive discussion of men's rights, borrowed chiefly from Thomas Rutherforth. Like Rutherforth, Paley divided rights into "natural or adventitious," "alienable or unalienable," and "perfect or imperfect," and invoked these distinctions at critical points in his discussion of morals and politics.⁵ For Paley, "expedient" did not clash with "just" or "right"; instead he employed the term to mean, as in the second definition of the *Oxford English Dictionary*, "conducive to advantage in general, or to a definite purpose; fit, proper, or suitable to the circumstances of the case."⁶ This definition followed closely Paley's central dictum that expediency was the means, and happiness the end of moral man in a moral society.

Thus, natural theology formed the basis of Paley's utilitarian moral theory and ultimately his political thought. From a careful scrutiny of God's works, men could discover a precept which should direct their moral deliberations; and this inference, drawn from the anatomical structure of natural phenomena, determined the moral obligation of men, as egoistic creatures, to the general felicity of their society. This logic, like so much else in Paley, was shared by a number of his predecessors.

III

The sources of Paley's theological utilitarianism have generally been traced to a scattered group of eighteenth-century ethicists that include John Gay, Daniel Waterland, and Abraham Tucker. Although Paley's knowledge of Waterland remains problematical, he certainly read Gay, whose short treatise on ethics appeared in 1731 as a preface to a work edited by Edmund Law, Paley's early patron and the father of his closest friend. Paley followed Gay in his definition of virtue, his psychological egoism, and in a number of minor features of his utilitarianism, though Paley tended to be less deterministic in his descriptions of human nature than the more mechanistic Gay. As some scholars have noted, Gay's brief essay influenced both the mechanistic philosopher David Hartley and Abraham Tucker, the usually cited immediate forerunner of Paley.[7]

Tucker, writing under the pseudonym Edmund Search, published his massive *The Light of Nature Pursued* between 1768 and 1778. Paley commends the work in the preface to his *Principles*, acknowledging it as the origin of much of his own thinking (pp. xv–xvi). Indeed, Leslie Stephen believes the two theories are identical and takes a curious personal liking to Tucker—by all accounts a charming eccentric—much at the expense of Paley, whom he treats with sardonic contempt.[8] As others have demonstrated, however, Paley's debt to Tucker was less comprehensive than Stephen suggests. To be sure, Paley followed the general bent of Tucker's theological utilitarianism, but the vast mass of Tucker's ponderous and often indescribably tedious work finds no parallel in the *Principles*. In fact, on specific points, Paley borrowed far more from the Cambridge divine Thomas Rutherforth, whom because of a private feud he never acknowledged, than from Tucker.[9]

Setting aside these quibbles over the specific derivation of ideas, however, one point remains clear. The theological utilitarians forthrightly rejected the notion of an independent moral sense, arguing in sound Lockean fashion that nothing could be innate to the mind and warning that, as Paley expressed it, "a system of morality, built upon instincts, will only find out reasons and excuses for opinions and practices already established, [and] will seldom correct or reform either" (p. 13). Because of this stance, it has been customary to distinguish the theological utilitarians from the Moral Sense school—from those ethicists like the Earl of Shaftesbury, Francis Hutcheson, Adam Smith, and, to some degree, Bishop Butler, who grounded morality on an inherent mechanism which directed moral deliberations.

Yet this undeniable distinction obscures as much as it enlightens. As we shall see, the Moral Sense school, no less than the theological utilitarians, were dependent upon the teleological categories of natural theology for their reflections on ethics. Natural religion provided them with a moral standard and, equally important, a methodology that often formed the intellectual armature of their analyses. If there were significant differences between the moral thought of, say, Paley and Shaftesbury, the bond between them was equally strong. It is as important to recognize the broad consensus between disparate thinkers of the Enlightenment, as it is to underscore their disagreements. Only then will Paley's utilitarianism emerge as the reflection of that consensus rather than the product of one or two isolated influences.

Anthony Ashley Cooper, the Earl of Shaftesbury, published his *Characteristics* in 1711. His optimism, his belief in the general harmony of nature, and his faith in man's benevolence have long been noted.[10] Less recognized, however, has been the role of teleological reasoning in the formation of these theories. In his analysis of morals, Shaftesbury wanted first of all to avoid the nemesis of most natural theologians, the composition fallacy. "To what End in Nature many things, even whole Species of Creatures, refer," he cautioned, ". . . will be hard for any-one justly to determine: But to what End the many Proportions and various Shapes of Parts in many Creatures actually serve; we are able, by the help of Study and Observation, to demonstrate with great exactness."[11] Shaftesbury viewed his own study as empirical, but it was of a fundamentally Aristotelian form; "the various shapes of Parts in many Creatures" were approached by finding their purpose rather than their efficient cause. Thus, he spoke of each person having a "private Good and Interest of his own, which Nature has compelled him to seek" and "a certain end in which every thing in his Constitution must *naturally* refer."[12] This end was happiness, which Shaftesbury recognized as a uniting factor of all moralists and indeed all men. To determine that there must be some mechanism within us to account for our benevolent affections, he employed the analogical reasoning of final cause.

> . . . an *Eye*, in its natural State, fails not to shut together of its own accord, unknowingly to us, by a peculiar Caution and Timidity; which if it wanted however we might intend the Preservation of our Eye, we should not in effect be able to preserve it, by any Observation or Forecast of our own. To be wanting therefore in those principal affections, which respect the Good of the whole Constitution, must be a Vice and Imperfection, as great surely in the principal parts, (the Soul or Temper) as it is in any of those inferior and subordinate parts, to want the self-preserving Affections which are proper to them.[13]

This mechanism Shaftesbury called the moral sense, though he offered only a fragmented and often misleading definition of it.

It was left to Francis Hutcheson, the Scottish philosopher who heavily influenced Hume, to develop more fully the moral sense theory. In *A System of Moral Philosophy*, published posthumously in 1755, Hutcheson declared that

> the intention of Moral Philosophy is to direct men to that course of action which tends most effectively to promote their greatest happiness and perfections; as far as it can be

done by observations and conclusions discoverable from the constitution of nature, without any aids of supernatural revelation.[14]

In other words, Hutcheson's utilitarianism derived empirically from the analogue of nature and excluded the dictates of revelation. Invoking the argument from design, he asserted that "God the Author . . . plainly intended the universal happiness and that of each individual, as far as it is consistent with it"; and he concluded that "this intention should be our rule."[15] Like Shaftesbury, he argued that there must be something in our nature which "judges about the means of subordinate ends" when confronted with perplexing moral difficulties. But, in an interesting deviation from Shaftesbury, he declared that "we must conceive in a Deity some *perceptive power* analogous to our *moral sense.*"[16] Thus, he argued analogically both from a God-created nature to man and then, conversely, from a quality of man back up to God. Moreover, this circularity persisted when Hutcheson framed his theodicy later in the book. "The whole inward constitution of the affections and *moral faculty,*" he declared, "is obviously contrived for the universal good"; and since the most judicious manner to judge a contrivance was by "the *proper end* or *effect,*" evil was not innate to man's nature.[17]

For Adam Smith, whose *Theory of Moral Sentiments* shared a number of key concepts with the Moral Sense school, teleological reasoning played an equally critical role. Here again the analogue of nature pointed toward the "happiness of mankind" as the "original purpose intended by the author of nature," since "no other end seems worthy of that supreme wisdom and divine benignity." By acting according to the dictates of our moral faculties, Smith said, echoing Shaftesbury and Hutcheson, "we necessarily pursue the most effectual means for promoting the happiness of mankind, and . . . advance as far as in our power the plan of Providence." A problem emerged, however, when he argued that gratitude or resentment should depend on the moral intention of the agent, since "in all ages the complaint and . . . great discouragement of virtue" has been "that the world judges by the event and not by the design."[18] Smith reconciled this difficulty by reverting once again to teleological categories.

> It is even of use that the evil which is done without design should be regarded as a misfortune to the doer as well as to the sufferer. Man is thereby taught to reverence the happiness of his brethren, to tremble lest he should, even unknowingly, do any thing that can hurt them, and to dread the animal resentment which he feels is ready to burst out against him, if he should without design be the unhappy instrument of their calamity.[19]

Characteristically rhetorical, this solution illustrated Smith's tendency to uncover the origin of a phenomenon by first seeking its purpose or final cause. If this procedure occasionally resulted in awkward tautologies, it also bound his ethics to natural religion.

Finally, the pervasive use of teleological categories in the framing of Enlightenment ethics can be illustrated by examining the links between Paley and Bishop Butler, the most thoroughgoing analogical reasoner of the century and one of its greatest moralists. In contrasting the two thinkers, the nineteenth-century logician William Whewell once observed that Paley was the moralist of utility and Butler of conscience.[20] Though fundamentally accurate, this contrast neglected the underlying similarities between the two great apologists. Thus, for example, Butler, like Paley, explicitly compared the hedonistic impulse to certain final causes in nature: "Just as the manifold appearances of design and final causes in the constitution of the world prove it to be the work of an intelligent Mind; so the particular final causes of pleasure and pain distributed amongst his creatures, prove that they are under His government."[21] This analogical linkage between natural theology and the central value of utilitarianism compared more favorably with Paley's method than did the more mechanistic approach of Gay or Tucker. And there were other similarities as well. Both wished to restore revelation to morals; both viewed the afterlife as the telic goal of secular living; both emphasized the cultivation of noble habits; and both conceived of religion in highly practical terms. Most important, it was Butler's persistent invocation of analogy—a method he called "natural, just, and conclusive"—that Paley faithfully followed. When Butler deemed the ultimate end of nature and providence to be "the most virtue and happiness possible,"[22] he was suggesting what eventually became the famous utilitarian formula for ethics and politics, a formula shared implicitly by a bevy of moralists not usually classed as utilitarian.

Thus, for many eighteenth-century moralists, the pursuit of happiness stemmed from a reading of God's work in nature. He created the universe benevolently, and, by analogy, men should direct their lives to their own happiness and the happiness of others. The concept of utility, which logically need not follow from happiness—someone may be happy without being useful and useful without being happy—derived from the application of final cause in nature to that of man. In nature, it was the adaption of ends to means which rendered a contrivance useful within its own context, and within the context of other contrivances. By analogy, it was the adaptations of ends to means in human nature—for example, the moral sense, or simply the implicit recognition that personal felicity may depend on that of others—which informed men of the needs of others and the path to salvation. Although there were substantial differences in both conception and detail between the two schools of thought, they were united in their application of teleological reasoning to the baffling questions of ethics.

Paley's *Principles* was thus not only the product of a handful of predecessors, but the reflection of a larger ethical consensus. Natural theology was the core of his ethical thinking, just as it was for ethicists as diverse as Abraham Tucker and Adam Smith. In an era famed for satire and bitter polemic, moralists conducted their discussions and debates with one another on a high level of mutual respect and intellectual sophistication precisely because they operated within a broad ideological consensus. As a writer late in the century, Paley distilled this consensus into a masterful synthesis that captured the essential unity of moral thought in the British Enlightenment.

IV

The doctrine of expediency was the central principle of Paley's ethics, reflecting his knowledge of natural theology and shaping his attitude to the concrete and practical moral problems that marked his real interest. To Paley, ethics was "that science which teaches men their duty, and the reasons of it" (p. 1), and consequently he devoted the largest portion of his *Principles* to an extended analysis of men's specific rights and their duties to themselves, their society, and God. This discussion, which consumes almost half the book, contains the bulk of his technical advice on such topics as business contracts, probate, legal oaths, and the duties of prayer. Since these sections defy easy recapitulation, it is best to sample Paley's moral beliefs by examining his stance on three key issues—private property, charity, and the problems of marriage and the family.

Certainly one of the most curious sections in all Paley's works is his opening discussion, "Of Property," in book three of the *Principles*. Rather than offering a customary exposition of its origins and development—a stock procedure since Hobbes—he chose to employ an imaginative analogy which almost immediately outraged his contemporaries and labeled him indelibly as "pigeon Paley":

> If you should see a flock of pigeons in a field of corn; and if (instead of each picking where and what it liked, taking just as much as it wanted, and no more) you should see ninety-nine of them gathering all they got, into a heap; reserving nothing for themselves, but the chaff and the refuse; keeping this heap for one, and that the weakest, perhaps worst, pigeon of the flock; sitting round and looking on, all the winter, whilst this one was devouring, throwing about, and wasting it; and if a pigeon more hardy or hungry than the rest, touched a grain of the hoard, all the others instantly flying upon it, and tearing it to pieces; if you should see this, you would see nothing more than what is every day practiced and established among men. Among men, you see the ninety-and-nine toiling and scraping together a heap of superfluities for one (and this one too, oftentimes the feeblest and worst of the whole set, a child, a woman, a madman, or a fool); getting nothing for themselves all the while, but a little of the coarsest of the provision, which their own industry produces; looking quietly on, while they see the fruits of all their labour spent or spoiled; and if one of the number take or touch a particle of the hoard, the others joining against him, and hanging him for the theft. [Pp. 72–73]

Wrenched out of context, this passage was, perhaps, the most radical declaration against property of the Enlightenment; Marx would have concurred with it, as would have most nineteenth-century socialists. It was the most passionate utterance in Paley's work and one he refused to eliminate at the bidding of his friend John Law, who predicted it would cost him a bishopric.[23]

Yet, the explicit antiaristocratic bias of the pigeon analogy was not without parallel in Paley's ethical thought. By emphasizing virtues that could be practiced by rich and poor alike, his definition of happiness was fundamentally democratic in character and, if anything, reflected his personal acceptance of the New Testament's occasional prejudice against wealth and privilege. "How hard it will be for those who have riches to enter the kingdom of God," Jesus told his disciples in the Gospel of Mark.[24] Paley saved some of his most scathing indictments for the idle preoccupations of certain members of the leisure class. "I have commonly remarked in such men," he wrote, "a restless and inextinguishable passion for variety; a great part of their time to be vacant, and so much of it irksome" (pp. 17–18). In both the pigeon analogy and his definition of happiness, then, Paley contributed to the growing polemic against aristocracies that arose in both Europe and America in the late eighteenth century—a polemic that has been skillfully documented by R. R. Palmer in his masterly *The Age of the Democratic Revolution.*[25]

Yet, as we shall see in his politics, Paley never wanted to unseat the aristocracy from political power, or to reform radically any of what Palmer has called its "constituted bodies": Parliament, the church, legal guilds, magistrates, and others who determined the character of the social order. The pigeon analogy demonstrated that Paley was painfully aware of the human exploitation that constituted the driving engine of private property; and this awareness, if taken in isolation, might endear him to Marxists and other debunkers of the English liberal tradition. But—to invoke Robert Walpole's remarkable self-characterization—Paley was "no Saint, no Spartan, no Reformer." He thought of himself instead as a political realist and man of common sense who, above all, prized social order and stability, and who endeavored to explicate the intricate mechanism of society, rather than condemn and overthrow it.

Thus, if the institution of private property embodied unsavory elements, there must be some reason, some larger purpose and design, which would justify its continuing

existence. "There must be some very important advantages to account for an institution which . . . is so para-
doxical and unnatural" (p. 73), Paley explained in the
section immediately following the analogy. He then proceeded to list every standard justification for the institution current in the eighteenth century, adding original
suggestions of his own. These included its tendency to
increase the productivity of land, to eliminate internal
strife over landownership in common, and to improve
"the conveniency of living" through a rational division of
labor. "The balance . . .," he concluded in weighing up his
arguments, "must preponderate in favour of property
with a manifest and great excess" (pp. 73–75). In effect, he
justified the institution on the basis of its expediency for
society, and his opening parable, striking in its stark per-
ception of human depravity, served as a rhetorical device
to initiate a dialectical argument with his readers, much
as he had done with his students at Cambridge.

But utility alone was not the sole grounds for possessing
large tracts of land. "It is the intention of God, that the
produce of the earth be applied to the use of man," he
declared; "this intention cannot be fulfilled without establishing property; it is consistent, therefore, with his
will, that property be established" (p. 80). Since this institution was consequently protected by the law of nature,
it followed that "a man has a right to keep and take every
thing which law will allow him to keep and take; which in
many cases will authorize the most flagitious chicanery"
(p. 81). He thus sanctioned philosophically the moral right
of unlimited possessive individualism, thereby granting
respectability to the "one, oftentimes the feeblest and
worst of the whole set," for whom the other ninety-and-
nine toiled.

If, with the exception of the pigeon analogy, Paley's
apology for private property seemed unrelentingly hostile
and insensitive to the needs of the poor, his attitude

toward individual and public charity was much more compassionate and humane. Charity he defined somewhat condescendingly as "promoting the happiness of our inferiors" (p. 153) and, in a passage reminiscent of the earlier and less sophisticated natural theologies of John Ray and William Derham, related the emotion of pity to the unfathomable wisdom of a great Creator:

> Whether it be an instinct or a habit, it is in fact a property of our nature, which God appointed; and the final cause for which it was appointed, is to afford to the miserable, in the compassion of their fellow-creatures, a remedy for those inequalities and distresses which God foresaw that many must be exposed to, under every general rule for the distribution of property. [P. 162]

To Paley, men labored under a strong obligation to relieve the distress of the poor, especially since all land was once held in common, the private possession of no single individual or state. He made it clear, however, that the primitive communism of the early Christians need provide "no precedent for our imitation" (p. 165); there were numerous possibilities for charitable offerings short of such drastic action. He was particularly incensed, however, at "the pretences by which men excuse themselves from giving to the poor" (p. 169); and to each of twelve common excuses, he retaliated with a strongly worded moral condemnation. Thus, to the pretense "that the poor do not suffer so much as we imagine; that education and habit have reconciled them to the evils of their condition," he angrily replied that "habit can never reconcile human nature to the extremities of cold, hunger, and thirst, any more than it can reconcile the hand to the touch of a red-hot iron." To Paley, "pride or prudery, or delicacy, or love of ease, keep one half of the world out of the way of observing what the other half suffer" (pp. 170–71).

On the problems of marriage and the family, Paley was equally forthright. He devoted an entire section of the *Principles* to the "Relative Duties which Result from the Constitution of the Sexes, and the Crimes opposed to these"—one of the few moralists in English philosophy to treat these social problems—and provided extensive discussions of fornication, seduction, adultery, incest, and polygamy (pp. 191–212). As a clergyman, he had had parishioners confide in him on some of these matters; and as a North Countryman whose attitude toward sex preserved the vitality of a Squire Weston, he brought to the discussion his usual healthy optimism.

His approach was nevertheless self-consciously utilitarian; he condemned sexual intercourse prior to marriage because "the male part of the species will not undertake the encumbrance, expense, and restraint of married life, if they can gratify their passions at a cheaper price; and they will undertake any thing, rather than not gratify them" (p. 193). On polygamy, he substantiated his criticism with the evidence of teleology:

> The equality in the number of males and females born into the world, intimates the intention of God, that one woman should be assigned to one man: for if to one man be allowed an exclusive right to five or more women, four or more men must be deprived of the exclusive possession of any; which could never be the order intended. [P. 208]

As in his earlier discussions of honesty and legal oaths, he never invoked an inviolable standard of right or wrong; his reasons always centered on the "tendency" of any action to contribute to or diminish the welfare of society.

Yet, as in his analysis of property, he often presented the stance of abstract utility, only to reject it on practical grounds. Thus, for example, he frankly admitted that he could find nothing in the marriage contract which "essentially distinguishes it from other contracts" and thereby rendered it incapable "of being dissolved by the consent of the parties, at the option of one of them, or either of them" (p. 214). Moreover, by actively eliminating the possibility of divorce, each marriage partner would be forced to remain compatible with the other:

> A man and woman in love with each other do this insensibly; but love is neither general nor durable: and where that is wanting, no lessons of duty, no delicacy of sentiment will go half so far with the generality of mankind and womenkind as this one intelligible reflection, that they must each make the best of their bargain; and that, seeing they must either both be miserable, or both share in the same happiness, neither can find their own comfort, but in promoting the pleasure of the other. [P. 215]

Moreover, if divorce laws were weakened, libertinism would batter and destroy a central prop in England's social stability—the enduring cement of a vigorous family life.

In his analysis of property, charity, and marriage, Paley therefore maintained a sturdy distrust of abstraction, preferring, much like Burke, those forms and institutions of society which had demonstrated their usefulness. He established a dialectic between the conclusions of pure reasoning and the facts of social utility. Thus, for example, although the institution of property did lead to an unfair distribution of goods—the lesson of the pigeon analogy—its concrete advantages to society far outweighed any theoretical abuse of human rights. Paley was consequently a man of practical imagination who, like the natural theologian delineating the final cause of a mechanism of nature, determined the function of a social norm before assigning it any moral value. If this mode of thought narrowed his vision and obscured the possibilities of genuine social progress, it also embodied a refreshing willingness to accept men without pretensions, simply as they were. Nowhere was this clearer than in his politics.

V

In their quest for a stable foundation of political obligation, Enlightenment theorists often initiated their analysis with a discussion of the origins of civil society. Once establish the rationale of political groupings, it was reasoned, and the rights and duties of both the citizen and government would follow, like postulates from a theorem. This preoccupation with origins, which never pretended to be historical in either its assumptions or methodology, had its counterpart in ethics, of course, where, as in Locke, moral problems were ultimately traced back to epistemology, ethics thereby becoming rooted in the fertile soil of human psychology. Only the rationalists dissented from this movement, and they, like the Cartesian physicists of the early eighteenth century, soon became isolated voices.

For some utilitarians, this procedure proved to be a mixed blessing. In ethics, it meant that moral obligation soon erupted as a critically important issue, since ethics had suddenly been cast adrift from the shorings of theology. Paley thought he avoided the difficulty by his definition of virtue, but for Bentham and the Philosophic Radicals it remained a contested issue through much of the nineteenth century. In politics, however, the central precepts of the utilitarians liberated them from the awkward fiction of the social contract which, by the late eighteenth century, had sustained damaging critical assaults from thinkers as diverse as Hume and Paley. Both substituted for its fictions the realities of how men actually behaved in political situations.

Paley rejected the social contract for two reasons. First, he questioned its historical reliability, arguing that only in America had there been anything resembling a gathering of free individuals to draw up a plan for future government. Second, and more important, he repudiated the notion that political obligations were passed from one generation to another without the knowledge or consent of those directly affected by them. "In all stipulations," he wrote, ". . . the parties must both possess the liberty of assent and refusal, and also be conscious of this liberty"; otherwise, all claims to allegiance were "vain and erroneous" (p. 336). As a theologian whose writings often implicitly challenged the binding condemnation of the Fall of Man, he instinctively mistrusted the authority of any abstract, legal fiction. If, as Locke suggested, man was born a *tabula rasa*, it was contradictory to bind him by the unsubstantiated promises of his forefathers.

In place of the social contract, Paley traced the origin of government to the gradual extension of the family unit into a protective military organization where "a warrior who had led forth his tribe against their enemies with repeated success, would procure to himself, even in the deliberations of peace, a powerful and permanent influence" (p. 322). He posited therefore that the first governments were probably monarchies, though he made it clear that this evolution carried with it no current rights or obligations for the citizen. His natural history of civil society thus resembled those in vogue among Scottish philosophers, and forecast in embryonic form the anthropological studies of primitive societies in the late nineteenth century. Both conceived of their tasks as essentially descriptive in character.

For this reason, Paley laid the groundwork for his discussion of political obligation by analyzing how, in fact, governments maintained control over their subjects. Since the physical strength of any nation ultimately resided in the governed, the question became why major revolutions were not more frequent and minor revolts even more violent. Writing four years before the French Revolution, Paley considered three possibilities. First, men obeyed from prejudice and prescription; "in monarchies and aristocracies which are hereditary, the prescription operates in favor of particular families; in republics and elective offices, in favor of particular forms of government, or constitutions" (p. 326). To Burke, the notion of "prescription" embodied almost mystic overtones and largely accounted for the permanence and stability of an organic state. To Paley, however, prescription was simply the habit of obedience that was not easily interrupted or broken. Second, men obeyed from "reason; that is to say, from conscience as instructed by reasonings and conclusions of their own." And finally, they obeyed from self-interest or "principally by fear, foreseeing that they would bring themselves by resistance into a worse situation than their present" (pp. 328–29).

Like Burke, Paley admonished those reformers who would impose uniformity upon government. "Some absurdities are to be retained," he declared, "and many small inconveniences endured in every country, rather than that the usage should be violated, or the course of public affairs diverted from their old and smooth channel." More important, "as ignorance of union, and want of communication, appear amongst the principal preservatives of civil authority, it behooves every state to keep its subjects in this want and ignorance." Paley hoped to prevent assemblies and the formation of combinations because he knew "the worst effect of popular tumults" was that the mass of men would discover their own strength (pp. 329–31). A large part of his veneration for English government centered on its tested ability to keep the citizens under control. For all his concern for the poor, he still regarded them as an unknown quantity in his political calculations.

More important, the moral basis of political obligation lay in the same standard that animated his ethics, "the Will of God as Collected from Expediency" (p. 339). Just as in nature, where each part of a contrivance contributed to the efficient functioning of the whole, so in politics each individual needed to fit his own interests and abilities to the happiness of the larger society. Conversely, a government was legitimate only as long as it could effectively serve its constituents, and therefore, as in Locke, the right of resistance became a crucial element in Paley's theory.

To Paley, the right of resistance was determined by the same type of mathematical procedure employed in ethics. Consequently, "the justice of every particular case of resistance [was] reduced to a computation of the quantity of the danger and grievance on the one side, and of the probability and expense of redressing it on the other" (p. 340). He carefully listed the significant factors to be evaluated when drawing up such a calculation, arguing that the interest of the whole society was binding upon every part of it. As in his extended analysis of evil in *Natural Theology*, no single exception ever disproved a general rule; the whole was always greater than the sum of its parts. Thus, just as teeth were not contrived to ache, so also political subjects were not intended to revolt—even though occasionally teeth ached and men revolted. The point of his discussion was that acts of political resistance, like occurrences of evil in nature, could take place only in extraordinary situations. Even the rebellion of the American colonies, tacitly supported by Edmund Burke, stirred uneasy feelings in Paley.

> Had I been an American, I should not have thought it enough to have had it even demonstrated, that a separation from the parent-state would produce effects beneficial to America: my relation to that state imposed upon me a farther inquiry, namely, whether the whole happiness of the empire was likely to be promoted by such a measure: not indeed the happiness of every part; that was not necessary, nor to be expected;—but whether what Great Britain would lose by the separation, was likely to be compensated to the joint stock of happiness, by the advantages which America would receive from it. [P. 345]

Like his "Reasons for Contentment," this analysis again made it clear that Paley was least effective in diagnosing or understanding the intense passions of political movements. He continually operated on the assumption that groups of men acted and responded like individuals—that the collective process of thought in the American colonies was not unlike his own ethical ruminations in Carlisle.

Yet, if some of his discussion failed to take adequate account of the dark recesses of political passion, other parts were much more illuminating. Three chapters in particular—"Of the British Constitution," "Of Crimes and Punishments," and "Of Religious Establishments and Toleration"—revealed Paley as a shrewd observer of the political process and established him as a formidable theorist who was to be quoted with respect in the House of Commons.[26]

Like Paine, his future adversary, Paley recognized that the British constitution consisted of no more than a complex series of legal precedents fabricated by men and always, therefore, subject to periodic revision. As a human and fallible artifact constructed over a period of time, it nevertheless drew its purpose and beauty from the dictates of God as revealed in nature. "There is one end of civil government peculiar to a good constitution," he wrote, and that was "the happiness of its subjects." The British constitution fulfilled this noble ideal and was the pride of Europe because all types of government achieved concrete expression in its various branches—"the monarchy residing in the King; the aristocracy, in the House of Lords; and the republic, being represented by the House of Commons" (pp. 377–78).

Paley thus conceived of the British constitution as an intricate network of checks and balances, each with its own particular purpose and each contributing to the efficient functioning of the whole. Specifically, this meant that it consisted of both a balance of power and a balance of interests. No single group could abuse its privilege without being "checked by some antagonist power residing in another part," while "the three estates of the empire are so disposed and adjusted, that whichever of the three shall attempt any encroachment, the other two will unite in resisting it" (pp. 384, 386). It functioned similarly to the famous watch of the *Natural Theology;* all its constituent parts made a meaningful contribution to the smooth operation of the entire machine of government.

Up to this point, Paley's discussion of the British Constitution displayed no remarkable qualities, save the author's characteristic lucidity. The notion of a balanced constitution, with its emphasis on the separation of powers, was the conventional wisdom of numerous eighteenth-century political commentators who, with varying degrees of clarity and coherence, elevated the doctrine into a kind of sacred writ. Montesquieu offered a classic exposition of the idea in *The Spirit of the Laws*, a work that enjoyed an enormous vogue in England. William Blackstone expanded and refined Montesquieu's analysis and, between 1765 and 1769, delivered to the world a seemingly impregnable monument of gentlemanly erudition, the *Commentaries on the Laws of England*. In 1776, the young Jeremy Bentham hurled his *Fragment on Government* against this monument, but no one much noticed. For if the four volumes of Blackstone proved too imposing to the patriotic Englishman, he could turn either to Jean Louis Delolme's *Constitution of England*, a popular interpretation of Montesquieu that was translated from the French in 1775, or, after 1785, to the *Principles* itself.[27]

But Paley's analysis of the British constitution was something more than a reiteration of trusted themes. Embodied in his discussion were two observations that set him apart from most of his distinguished forerunners.[28] The first of these concerned the function of crown patronage in maintaining the balanced constitution. Paley claimed that without an extensive system of patronage in his firm control, the king would soon relinquish much of his political power to the House of Commons. To illustrate his case, he argued that Britain ultimately lost the American colonies because "the king and government of Great Britain held no patronage in [America], which would create attachment and influence sufficient to counteract that restless arrogating spirit, which, in popular assemblies, when left to itself, will never brook an authority that checks and interferes with its own" (p. 397). When the *Principles* was published in 1785, it had been only five years since the passage of the famous Dunning resolution that "the influence of the crown has increased, is increasing, and ought to be diminished" and only three years since Burke's bill for economical reform had eliminated some of the more outrageous governmental sinecures. Paley did not defend all forms of patronage: he allowed that "superfluous and exorbitant emoluments of office" should be abolished (p. 395). He sensed, however, that the future lay overwhelmingly with the House of Commons and he quoted with approval the "much decried apophthegm" that " 'an independent parliament is incompatible with the existence of the monarchy' " (p. 400).

There was little in Montesquieu, Blackstone, Delolme, or even Burke that parallels this appraisal of the political significance of the patronage system. But there was at least one observer who posited the same argument and, considering the bulk of Paley's writings on religion, it is not without irony that on this political point the two should agree. In an essay entitled "Of the Independency of Parliament," David Hume argued that the patronage of the crown, whether it was called "influence" or "by the invidious appellations of *corruption* and *dependence*," was nevertheless "inseparable from the very nature of the constitution, and necessary to the preservation of our mixed government."[29] Both Paley and Hume based their case for the preservation of a mixed constitution less upon the theoretical, legal, and historical arguments summoned up by most political philosophers than upon the pragmatic expedient of a functioning system of patronage.[30] On this issue, the two adversaries who never met were linked by their uncompromising realism.

A second aspect of Paley's political thought that signaled something of a departure from traditional allies such as Montesquieu, Blackstone, Delolme, and Burke centered on a notion that initially might seem awkward coming from an avowed utilitarian. In discussing the role played by reform in shaping the British constitution, Paley advanced the idea that

> political innovations commonly produce many effects beside those that are intended. The direct consequence is often the least important. Incidental, remote, and unthought-of evil or advantages, frequently exceed the good that is designed, or the mischief that is forseen. It is from the silent and unobserved operation, from the obscure progress of causes set at work for different purposes, that the greatest revolutions take their rise. [P. 375]

Paley reached back into English history to buttress his claim. Thus, for example, Queen Elizabeth had unwittingly contributed to the growth of a strong, oligarchical House of Commons when she helped enact laws that encouraged commerce and trade. In politics, Paley reaffirmed, "the most important and permanent effects have, for the most part, been incidental and unforeseen" (p. 377).

This doctrine of unintended consequences formed the theoretical superstructure of Paley's opposition to electoral reform. Ever since the protracted controversy over

John Wilkes in the 1760s and early 1770s, there had been voices clamoring for some alteration of the franchise. By the time of the American debacle, reformers had gathered support in high places. The young Pitt introduced moderate bills in 1782 and 1783, and though both efforts failed to impress a majority, the promise of reform had not been snuffed out. In 1785, Pitt, who was now the king's chief minister, presented a bill that among other things disenfranchised thirty-two rotten boroughs and transferred their votes to the new and rapidly expanding population centers. For any political commentator, even one as geographically isolated as Paley, the issue of electoral reform could not be avoided.

As in his analysis of property, Paley again resorted to a startling paradox to explain his position. "There is nothing in the British constitution so remarkable," he began, "as the irregularity of the popular representation."

> The House of Commons consists of five hundred and fifty-eight members, of whom two hundred are elected by seven thousand constituents; so that a majority of these seven thousand, without any reasonable title to superior weight or influence in the state, may, under certain circumstances, decide a question against the opinion of as many millions. [P. 390]

Like the pigeon analogy, this statement stood in splendid isolation from the remainder of his discussion, acting as a foil to his later thrusts against its radical implications.

For Paley was no democrat. He believed, as did Burke, that Parliament should represent only the landed and moneyed interests, or those who "counted" in English society. "If the country be not safe in such hands," he asked, "in whose may it confide its interests?" He rejected the notion that any man possessed "a natural right" to vote, adding in a jocular footnote that if such a right existed, women would be able to vote as well (pp. 392–93).

Though he defended the buying of seats as an effective means of introducing talent into the legislature, he condemned electoral bribery as a corrupting influence on enlightened government. Above all, he feared massive reform, warning that it would lead to the unintended consequence of mob rule. "No order or assembly of men whatever," he admonished, "can long maintain their place and authority in a mixed government, of which the members do not individually possess a respectable share of personal importance" (p. 393).

Ernest Barker once called Paley's chapter on the British constitution "a memorable page in the history of political theory."[31] Certainly Paley himself was proud of it; during the turbulent days after the outbreak of the French Revolution, he republished it as a separate pamphlet and distributed it among he poor, along with his "Reasons for Contentment." As in his analysis of "Rights and Duties," the chapter restated a number of conventional ideas—the notion of a mixed monarchy, for example—but it offered a genuine contribution to political thought by explaining in detail what other theorists grasped only in the abstract. In his analysis of the patronage system, for instance, he articulated clearly and distinctly the premises of eighteenth-century government as it actually operated, thereby linking himself with a handful of talented writers on English government in the Enlightenment.

Similar to his analysis of the British Constitution, Paley's chapter "Of Crimes and Punishments" confronted a topic of intense concern for many Englishmen. Ever since the middle of the eighteenth century, efforts at reforming the complex and often brutally ineffective system of penal law had attracted wide attention. For example, in *An Inquiry into the Causes of the Late Increase of Robbers*, published in 1750, the novelist Henry Fielding directed his considerable talent to the problem of crime prevention and was flattered when, a few years later, a committee appointed by the House of Commons recommended acceptance of some of his suggestions. In 1771, a young barrister named William Eden published his *Principles of Penal Law*, which, inspired by Montesquieu and the Italian jurist Beccaria, argued that the severity of punishment—particularly the wide use of the death penalty—rarely served as a deterrent to crime. Finally, it was during this same period, of course, that Jeremy Bentham began his long struggle for the complete revision of the English legal code.[32]

Paley was not insensitive to the insights of these legal reformers. Like Bentham and others, for example, he considered the function of punishment to be essentially pedagogical and didactic; its purpose was to prevent crime rather than simply penalize it. And, similar to Bentham's theory, it was to be strictly proportional, "the retribution of so much pain for so much guilt" in accordance with "the justness of God" and the utilitarian formula (p. 425). Yet, in a sharp departure from his brilliant contemporary, Paley did not view the existing legal system as corrupt or archaic. In some of the more remarkable passages of the *Principles*, he strongly defended the death penalty for the stealing of horses, sheep, and "cloth from tenters or bleaching grounds" because "property being more exposed, requires the terror of capital punishment to protect it" (pp. 427–28).

It soon became apparent, however, that he was not nearly so harsh as he appeared. "Of those who receive the sentence of death," he observed, "scarcely one in ten is executed" (p. 430). This statistic, which flabbergasted Bentham and illustrated for him the irrationality of English law,[33] convinced Paley that the existing penalties fulfilled an important function; "few actually suffer death," he wrote, "whilst the dread and danger of it hangs over the crimes of many" (p. 431). In keeping with its pedagogic principle, capital punishment thus served, like the execution of Admiral Byng, to "encourage" the others.

Though at one point Paley maintained prophetically that the certainty of punishment was of more consequence than its severity, he was deeply impressed by the efficacy of terror and fear in reforming criminals:

> If there be any thing that shakes the soul of a confirmed villain, it is the expectation of approaching death. The horrors of this situation may cause such a wrench in the mortal organs, as to give them a holding turn: and I think it probable, that many of those who are executed, would, if they were delivered at the point of death, retain such a remembrance of their sensations, as might preserve them . . . from relapsing into their former crimes. But this is an experiment that, from its nature, cannot be repeated often. [Pp. 440–41]

He argued firmly against public executions, pointing out that they hardened and depraved "the public feelings," but he expressed genuine interest in "the proposal, not long since suggested, of casting murderers into a den of wild beasts, where they would perish in a manner dreadful to the imagination, yet concealed from the view" (p. 444). Thus, although Paley himself considered his legal theory entirely consistent with his utilitarianism, it retained strong elements of revenge and retribution alien to the spirit of the reformers. Once again, he proved himself to be a frank apologist who for a generation would be a comfort to all opponents of legal reform.[34]

On the Established Church, his views differed from those of William Warburton, whose "Alliance of Church and State" was the locus classicus of orthodoxy in the eighteenth century. Writing in 1736, Warburton attempted to demonstrate that the contemporary arrangement between Church and State was in direct accordance

with Divine Providence; and he buttressed and orna-
mented this theme with detailed and sometimes fanciful
discussions on the social compact and the nature of cor-
porate societies.35 Paley followed a different tack. Apply-
ing the general principle which informed his entire analysis of politics and society, he justified an Established
Church solely on the grounds of utility, cautioning gravely
that every effort to make "the church an engine, or even an
ally, of the state . . . has served only to debase the institution and to introduce into it numerous corruptions
and abuses." To Paley, the Church had one purpose, one
final cause, and that was "the preservation and communication of religious knowledge" (p. 450).

To fulfill this end, it was necessary to maintain a large
clergy, adequately compensated for its services. In his
"Distinction of Orders in the Church Defended upon the
Principles of Public Utility," published in 1782, he
funneled his efforts into showing how the existing hierar-
chical structure filled a critical need in English society.
First, he argued that any organization demanded some
chain of command to govern and correct the behavior of its
members; "whatever may be the benefits of equality," he
asserted, "peace is best secured by subordination." Moreover, since the various distinctions within the Church of
England corresponded to those of civil society, they "supplied each class of the people with a clergy of their own
level and description, with whom they may live and associate upon terms of equality." Third, he argued that the
higher orders of the clergy lent the Church a dignity which
would be lost through leveling; as in law and the military,
the higher offices gleaned respect mainly from the "lustre
and esteem" which accompanied such exalted positions.
Finally, "rich and splendid situations in the church have
been justly regarded as prizes held out to invite persons of
good hopes and ingenious attainments to enter into ser-

vice."[36] That aspect of the Established Church usually most criticized—the plush preferments with their enormous stipends, political influence, palaces, and ill-defined responsibilities—Paley defended as an incentive for bright young clergy to become better Christians.

If, after his initial disagreement with Warburton, his views meshed comfortably with the orthodoxies of his age, his position on religious toleration was much more controversial. He distinguished between "partial toleration," where dissenters were allowed freedom of worship but excluded from public office, and "complete toleration," where all citizens were granted full civil rights. Manifesting the Latitudinarian influence of his Cambridge colleagues, many of whom vigorously protested against the imposed uniformity of the Thirty-nine Articles, Paley strongly advocated complete toleration. "I perceive no reason," he wrote, "why men of different religious persuasions may not sit upon the same bench, deliberate in the same council, or fight in the same ranks . . . as men of various or opposite opinions" (p. 473). To Paley, as to Locke before him and John Stuart Mill later on, only in the free marketplace of ideas could the best ideas emerge.

Paley's politics contained elements of both the controversial and the conventional, just as they combined both the abstract and the concrete in an often uneasy alliance. Like Bentham, he deduced the principle of utility from a standard outside the fields of ethics and politics, but unlike Bentham, he did not employ it to criticize existing institutions.[37] In ethics and in politics, Paley remained a practical theorist who, similar to the natural theologian, judged an institution by how well ends were adapted to means. Surveying the politics of his time, he saw only successes; whether it was in the British constitution with its unique pattern of checks and balances, or in the legal code with its inconsistent enforcement of the death penalty, he sought the rationale of existing practices.

VI

In summary, from the *Principles of Moral and Political Philosophy*, published in 1785, to the crowning achievement of his *Natural Theology*, published in 1802, everything Paley wrote was intimately related by a web of interlocking analogies that bound the various strands of his philosophy into a single fabric. The ancient and venerable argument from design occupied the center of this unity, exercising a powerful dominion over all his thought and solving a central problem of Enlightenment theology. By demonstrating the existence of God with evidence drawn from the latest scientific inquiries, the teleological argument united science and religion in a common endeavor that even the bold genius of David Hume could neither shatter nor deflect.

From this satisfying accomplishment in natural religion emanated the further challenge to go and do likewise for revealed religion, a challenge Paley met with two very different, but related works; the detailed and academic *Horae Paulinae* attacked the problem of forgery in the writings of St. Paul and was the rough equivalent of a modern scholarly monograph, while the more general and synthetic *Evidences of Christianity* restated the best thinking on the subject during the preceding century. Both works meshed logically with the final link in Paley's system, his ethical and political philosophy. As a theological utilitarian, he borrowed his notions of both "happiness" and "utility" from natural religion, where God's benevolence and will could be deduced from the skillful adaption of means to ends in biological contrivances.

Though it is perfectly proper to refer to Paley's "system," he was not a systemizer in the conventional sense. There was little in his writings that resembled scholasticism or seventeenth-century French rationalism, both of which Locke had impatiently dismissed in book three of his *Essay concerning Human Understanding.* Like the new scientists of the early Enlightenment, empiricists like Paley sought a plurality of laws that ordered and explicated the kaleidoscopic diversity of the external world, rather than a single, all-embracing synthesis that substituted metaphysical jargon for precise analysis. The simple fact that Paley composed his works in an order the reverse of that in which they were to be interpreted suggests that he approached his task in a spirit alien to the rationalism of a Samuel Clarke or a Richard Price.

Yet, just as the corpus of Hume's work can be taken as a systematic refutation of every major assumption and cherished idea of the British Enlightenment, so Paley's complete works can be seen as the reassertion of those same ideas, those same assumptions. It has been one of the theses of this study that the coherence of Paley's philosophy, its synthetic quality, reflected an ideological consensus among British intellectuals in the eighteenth century. As a former college lecturer whose task it once was to convey to a new generation of students the essential features of past thought, Paley distilled and crystallized the strategic ideas of his predecessors into a philosophy whose very comprehensiveness justified its modest claims to originality.

His *Natural Theology* mirrored the symbiotic relationship between science and religion that had sustained investigators from Boyle to Priestley. His two works of biblical criticism offered cogent explanations for the logical difficulties stemming from the assumptions and methodology that buttressed such an alliance—difficulties raised initially by the deists and further elaborated by Hume. Finally, with its emphasis on teleological categories, his ethics and politics reflected a broad agreement among British moralists that transcended their specific disputes over such issues as the existence of a moral sense.

CHAPTER 6

Paley and the Nineteenth Century

THE IMPACT OF PALEY'S WORKS ON THE NINETEENTH century assumed two different but related forms. First, since some of his early books were expanded and refined versions of his enormously popular lectures at Cambridge, the same qualities of mind he brought to the classroom— rigorous organization, unfailing clarity, and an essentially orthodox point of view—made his published efforts admirably suited for use in a university curriculum. Though tutors at Oxford often encouraged students to read Paley, it was at Cambridge in particular that his works became an institutionalized part of undergraduate education. The *Principles* was required of students as early as 1786 and remained part of the examination system well into the nineteenth century. The *Evidences* enjoyed even more lasting favor. As part of the Previous examination, or Little-go, required of all second-year undergraduates after 1822, it stayed on the examination list until 1920, when it was finally abandoned.[1] Until that time, every Cambridge undergraduate, in whatever subject, was expected to know something about Paley.

Yet, Paley's legacy to the nineteenth century rested not only on some required texts that, to some undergraduates, must have been a tiresome hurdle on the path to a university degree. As we have seen, Paley's works formed a unified corpus of thought that embodied many of the most treasured assumptions of the Enlightenment in England. It was this unity, this synthesis, that he bequeathed to the nineteenth century. His works provided an elegant and often intimidating model that thinkers for at least three decades after his death could imitate, alter, or reject, but not ignore. His impact on later intellectuals was sometimes direct and occasionally unacknowledged, and consequently the task of tracing Paley's changing influence involves something more than running down every reference to his name in the hundred years following his death. It also demands understanding how his integrated approach to philosophic problems and the assumptions which buttressed his solutions to these problems were either sustained or repudiated by various nineteenth-century thinkers.

If the cohesiveness and lucidity of Paley's philosophy proved attractive, however, many of his specific notions about theology and politics faced an almost immediate barrage of penetrating criticism. In ethics, the reestablishment of the moral sense and supremacy of conscience by both the Evangelicals and the Romantics eventually resulted in a sharp diminution of his influence, especially at Cambridge, the stronghold of the *Principles*. In revealed religion, the gradual encroachment of German historicism and biblical exegesis spelled doom for the Paleyan method of literary analysis, though the *Evidences* would be respected long after the *Principles* settled into peaceful oblivion. Only the *Natural Theology* avoided the barbs of carping critics, mainly because it embodied general principles and assumptions which nineteenth-century scientists and theologians found indispensable. Even after the deadly thrust of Darwin's *Origin of Species*, Paley's statement of the teleological argument stood as a model of confidence and clarity for thousands of Christians who lamented the threatened disintegration of their world-view.

Each of these themes deserves further exploration, starting with the *Principles*, whose influence was initially most powerful, but shortest lived. Only after an analysis of the specific fate of each of Paley's major works will it be possible to evaluate his niche in the cultural history of England and appreciate his achievement as a moralist and theologian.

II

The *Principles* occupied a crucial place in the Cambridge curriculum after 1786, when it was first introduced for use in examinations. "It would scarcely be believed," recalled George Pryme of Trinity in the late eighteenth century, "how very little knowledge was required for a degree when I first knew Cambridge. Two books of Euclid's geometry, simple and quadratic equations, and the early parts of Paley's *Moral Philosophy* were deemed amply sufficient."[2] Paley was so important to undergraduate education that by the mid-nineteenth century there had emerged a variety of study guides especially designed for harried students who, either from stupidity or laziness, sought to harvest the fruits of Paley's philosophy without protracted labor. One of the most popular, Thomas Coward's *Analysis,* contained not only a convenient outline of the book, but also a selection of previous examination questions. "How does Paley establish the position that the pleasures of ambition and superiority are common to all conditions? What are adventitious rights? How are they created?"—these were but a few of the questions which undergraduates pondered in the tense weeks before examinations.[3]

The *Principles* thus exercised a powerful intellectual

hegemony over a substantial portion of England's educated elite. "It has laid the foundation of the Moral Principles of many hundreds—probably thousands—of Youth while under a course of training designed to qualify them for being afterwards the Moral instructors of Millions," Richard Whately wrote in 1859; "such a work therefore cannot fail to exercise a very considerable and extensive influence over the Minds of successive generations."[4] The precise nature of this influence, however, remains difficult to estimate. It seems reasonable to assume that for a number of students a thorough knowledge of Paley at Cambridge provided them with a frame of mind amenable to a later acceptance of more secular forms of utilitarianism, but this assumption, though tantalizing, is difficult to prove. Perhaps the best way of assessing Paley's influence in the early part of the nineteenth century is to examine the numerous and often vicious attacks on the book—attacks whose very animus indicated the strength of Paley's text.

Between 1785 and 1830, the *Principles* and, in particular, the notion of expediency were assaulted by Christian writers from both outside and within the university. Leading this attack was a young Evangelical named Thomas Gisborne, whose *Principles of Moral Philosophy*, published in 1789, condemned Paley's key ethical concept as pernicious and unreliable. Expediency, Gisborne claimed, was not in the Bible; it led to rationalizations about our ethical responsibilities; its consequences could not be predicted by the moral agent. "General expediency is an instrument not to be wielded by a mortal hand," he warned his readers.[5]

Paley gained some defenders, but they were far outnumbered by such critics as Peter Roberts, Thomas Ludlam, and Thomas Green, who argued that expediency vitiated moral conscience and reduced men to calculating villains.[6] Following Gisborne's leadership, these observers condemnèd the doctrine as sanctioning the ethics of Mammon and the marketplace, and as the morality of barter rather than forgiveness. Already by 1800 many readers of the archdeacon would probably have agreed with Wilberforce that Gisborne had "fully established his charge against Paley, and [had] shown with great effect how little such a principle as general expediency is fit for man."[7]

For Coleridge, not only did Paley's natural theology represent "the utter rejection of all present and living communion with the universal Spirit"; his ethics and politics were an open declaration of moral bankruptcy. Narrow, superficial, and external, the doctrine of expediency was heathen rather than Christian. It was the triumph of a legalistic mind incapable of perceiving the subtleties of moral behavior and therefore blind to the essential mystery of human life. It signaled a "debasing slavery to the outward senses" which permitted men to indulge their sensual instincts while ignoring their Christian duties. It was, in short, an "all-settling scheme . . . which is the anarchy of morals."[8]

Although Coleridge diverted most of his energies into polemic, his passionate complaints against Paley bore a remarkable resemblance to the earlier denunciations of the Evangelicals. Both substituted an ethic of inward conscience and spiritual obligation for the abstract, rational, and materialistic moral system of Paley; and both viewed the English empiricists as shallow optimists mentally incapable of penetrating into the mystic depths of man and the universe.[9] If Coleridge drew most of his critique from German philosophy, his polemic against eighteenth-century ideas had another, more personal dimension: as a young man he had been strongly attracted to the philosophic materialism of David Hartley—he named his first son after him—and his later criticism of Paley and the materialists drew at least some of its bitterness from the disillusionment of a former convert severing himself from his past.

Yet, Coleridge was not the only Romantic who sharply castigated Paley. William Hazlitt considered the *Principles* "a disgrace to the national character" and a "cast-off, threadbare excuse" for immoral behavior. In his masterpiece of invective entitled "Of the Clerical Character," he dubbed it "a somewhat ingenious and amusing apology for existing abuses of every description," but he saved his heavy artillery for the personal character of Paley himself. "This same shuffling Divine," he began after recounting the Feather's Tavern episode, "is the same Dr. Paley, who afterwards employed the whole of his life, and his moderate second-hand abilities, in tampering with religion, morality, and politics—in trimming between his convenience and his conscience—in crawling between heaven and earth and trying to cajole both."[10]

Hostility to the *Principles* extended to respected dons at Cambridge itself. At Kings, the ascendancy of Charles Simeon meant that Evangelical mistrust of the archdeacon began filtering through to undergraduates,[11] while at Sidney Sussex, the master, Edward Pearson, openly proclaimed his disenchantment. His *Remarks on the Theory of Morals*, first published in 1800, included both a polemic against the Evangelicals and a detailed critique of the *Principles*, which, Pearson charged, omitted the moral sense and failed to distinguish between motive and obligation in its definition of virtue. Though some defenders rallied to Paley's aid—in 1830 Latham Wainewright directed a *Vindication of Dr. Paley's Theory of Morals* against Pearson and the Evangelical Gisborne—by the time Coleridge's theological reflections were gaining wide currency among Cambridge undergraduates in the late 1820s, Paley's moral thought had already felt the bite of vigorous revaluation.[12]

What finally broke the hegemony of the *Principles*, however, was its repudiation by a small but enormously powerful group of Cambridge thinkers who, inspired by the rising star of Coleridge, despised utilitarianism and wished its influence swept from the university. [13] Their antipathy found one of its most powerful expressions in Adam Sedgwick's *Discourse on the Studies of the University*, a lecture delivered in December of 1832 and published the following year. Born in 1785, the year the *Principles* was published, Sedgwick was Fifth Wrangler in 1808 and soon after became a fellow of Trinity College. Despite frequent bouts of a mysterious illness—Sedgwick lived a long life fervently believing he was about to die—he was appointed Woodwardian Professor of Geology in 1818 and twelve years later earned entry into the Royal Society for his distinguished contributions to that young field. Temperamental and often outrageously unfair, Sedgwick constantly meddled in university affairs, generally on the side of reform; and though primarily a scientist, he was also keenly interested in the morals of his admiring students.[14] It was to this end that he composed the *Discourse*.

Sedgwick challenged Paley's utilitarianism because its "false reasoning" had "a degrading effect on the temper and conduct of those who adopted it." Though he acknowledged "reverence" for the man who "during his time [did] much more for the cause of revealed truth than any other writer of this country," Sedgwick vehemently protested against Paley's denial of the moral sense. "To reject the moral sense is to destroy the foundation of all moral philosophy," he argued; "virtue becomes a question of calculation—a matter of profit or loss: and if a man gain heaven at all on such a system, it must be by arithmetical details—the computation of his daily work—the balance of his moral ledger." Such ethics had "no common bond of union" with true Christianity and led "inevitably . . . to a

sordid and groveling life."[15] As with both Coleridge and
the Evangelicals, Sedgwick's distrust of Paley stemmed
from the fear that if left alone and to their own devices,
men would always sink into sin and immorality. Ethics
implied duty, struggle, a war on the senses; in the battle
against eternal damnation, the greatest threat came from
within.

What Adam Sedgwick asserted, William Whewell confirmed. One of the most powerful intellects of his age,
Whewell wrote confidently on mathematics, physics, logic,
history, and philosophy. In 1818 he had helped found the
Cambridge Philosophical Society and a year later published a textbook on mechanics which employed the new
Continental system of mathematics. In 1837 he issued his
magnum opus, *The History of the Inductive Sciences*, and a
year later was elected Knightsbridge Professor of Moral
Philosophy, the chair once held by Paley's mentor and
patron, Edmund Law. In 1838 he also published *On the
Foundation of Morals*, a highly rhetorical pamphlet whose
avowed purpose was the refutation of Paley's *Principles*.
Whewell advocated dropping the book from the curriculum "without further delay," claiming it was partially
responsible for "the confusion and vacillation of thought
. . . at present so generally prevalent in England." He returned to this theme in his *Elements of Morality*, published eight years later. "Expediency implies a way out
of difficulties," he averred, "but Morality places before us
a higher object than merely to escape from difficulties. She
teaches us to aim at what is right."[16]

Although Sedgwick and Whewell often opposed each
other on local issues of university reform, they were agreed
on the dangers and inadequacies of utilitarianism. The
combined assault by two of Cambridge's most distinguished professors discredited the *Principles* immeasur-
ably, and though it would remain on the reading lists of

some colleges far into the nineteenth century, its practical influence collapsed during the 1830s.

This repudiation posed a unique problem for John Stuart Mill, who disliked Paley but not, of course, the theory of utility. In 1835 he published a lengthy review of Sedgwick's *Discourse* in which he dismissed Paley's version of utilitarianism as ill-conceived, arbitrary, and ultimately shallow. "Of Paley's work, though it possesses in a high degree some minor merits, we think it on the whole meanly," he affirmed, and then continued by accusing Paley of lacking the "single-minded earnestness for truth" and "intrepid defiance of prejudice which the word 'philosopher' supposes."[17]

Though Mill rejected the theological utilitarianism of Paley, he was also anxious to defend the Benthamite version of utilitarianism against the broad volleys of Sedgwick. Here Mill showed himself in the full cloak of his youthful arrogance; Sedgwick was a "master of stockphrases" and "carried away by ambiguity"; his performance did "gross injustice even to Paley" and his work ranked as a popular book geared for a readership "with a lower class of capacities." Because "a doctrine is not judged at all until it is judged in its best form," the *Discourse* completely missed the mark; "Mr. Sedgwick has no right to represent Paley as a type of the theory of utility," Mill wrote contemptuously, and—from his tone—presumably no right to discuss ethics at all.[18]

Toward Whewell, Mill was equally hostile. In an article appearing in the *Westminster Review* of October 1852, he called the *Elements* "a catalogue of received opinions" and "one of the thousand waves on the dead sea of commonplace." To Mill, Whewell's emphasis on duty and rectitude represented a classic case of circular logic, but he nevertheless sadly acknowledged the coming of a new era at Cambridge, when utility was "abjured as deadly heresy,

and the doctrine of *a priori* or self-evident morality
. . . became the orthodox theory." As in his essay "Utilitarianism," Mill brilliantly defended the creed of his
childhood against its influential critics, making clear that
the principle of greatest happiness did not sanction a
hedonistic slide into immoral behavior. "We are as much
for conscience, duty, and rectitude as Dr. Whewell," he
concluded angrily.[19]

Though Sedgwick, Whewell, and their Cambridge allies
could not eradicate all forms of utilitarianism, they did
inflict on the *Principles* a mortal wound. Even Mill refused
to touch this discarded hulk. Yet, by 1840 the name of
William Paley was by no means a fading memory; his
ethical philosophy may have suffered from the repeated
blows of powerful opponents who righteously asserted the
supremacy of conscience, but his religious thought continued to be held in high esteem. In fact, if Cambridge
eventually became united in its rejection of expediency, it
was also at one in its admiration and emulation of Paley's
biblical criticism and especially his natural religion.

III

The *Evidences* ran through twenty-four editions by
1816 and became an official part of the Cambridge
curriculum in 1822, though it had appeared in undergraduate reading lists long before its formal adoption for
examinations. As in the case of the *Principles*, this inclusion
resulted in a number of "analyses" and "epitomes"
specifically designed for struggling students, and during
the course of the nineteenth century, over a score of these
crutches made their debut. Thus, for example, in 1836
Thomas Coward's *Analysis of Paley's Evidences of Christianity, with Examination Questions to Each Chapter* was
published; similar editions by other authors appeared in
1855, 1870, 1881, 1898, and 1910.[20] As late as 1898, Paley

retained vigorous defenders such as J. P. Taylor, who in a short pamphlet praised the archdeacon for his "practical wisdom" and "admirable good sense," while at the same time countering the prevailing charge that the *Evidences* was hopelessly old-fashioned.[21]

Though *Horae Paulinae* did not enjoy the spectacular success of the *Evidences*, it was by no means immediately forgotten; by 1819 it had gone through ten editions and spawned at least five supplements and epitomes. It is clear, then, that Paley's two works of biblical criticism lived healthily throughout the nineteenth century, surviving longer than his other productions. As late as 1909, a clever and anonymous "Paley's Ghost" composed *Paley Verses*, presumably for Christians who appreciated such lines as

> Miracles and actions true,
> The Author of the Acts Paul knew,
> The Epistles and the Acts agree
> Entirely undesignedly.[22]

Early in the nineteenth century, Paley's approach to revelation had been the model for such works as J. J. Blunt's *Undesigned Coincidences in the Writings Both of the Old and New Testament* and the Bampton lectures of both William Van Mildert and Henry Hart Milman.[23] Like his *Natural Theology*, Paley's *Evidences* elicited some of its strongest support from the leaders of the Broad Church movement, who, though they often disputed certain of his arguments, agreed with his underlying assumption that reason and revelation need not be antithetical.

Among the first generation of Broad Churchmen— Thomas Arnold, Julius Hare, Connop Thirlwall, Frederick Maurice, Richard Whately—Paley registered his most noticeable impact on Richard Whately, the Oxford-educated Archbishop of Dublin who in 1834 helped found the Statistical Society and there established contact with both

Malthus and other Cambridge notables. Like his brethren in Cambridge, Whately repudiated Paley's ethical system but embraced his Christian apologetics. Thus, in his edition of *Paley's Moral Philosophy* published in 1859, he faulted the archdeacon for eliminating the moral sense and advocated as a "safer guide" the intuitionist approach of Bishop Butler. In his edition of the *Evidences* published the same year, however, he warmly complimented Paley for providing a "sufficient" reason for Christian reliance on the Gospels. Unlike many other members of the Broad Church movement, Whately felt neither alarmed nor mentally invigorated by German metaphysics and biblical criticism. "The spectre will resolve itself into the old worn-out clothes of Collins and Toland and Chubb and Hume, which are too soiled and thread-bare to be exhibited in daylight," he said, dismissing the new schools of thought.[24]

Whately, in these two editions of Paley, and also in such educational productions as his *Christian Evidences: Intended Chiefly for the Young*, argued strongly for a rational inquiry into religious faith. Like Paley, he abhorred "the absurd extravagances into which some enthusiasts have fallen" and maintained that Christianity could easily withstand the acid test of objective analysis.[25] In his love of tolerance and rationality, his willingness to compromise, and his abiding hatred of enthusiasm, Whately shared the faith of the eighteenth century and was a natural ally of Paley's theology.

One year after Whately had rejected German criticism in his two editions of Paley, *Essays and Reviews* enthusiastically endorsed the German approach. Perhaps the best single statement of Broad Church principles in mid-Victorian England, *Essays and Reviews* can be seen as the logical completion of Coleridge's attempt to integrate German philosophy into the mainstream of English theology.[26] Its subsequent condemnation showed that orthodox divines were not yet prepared to jettison some of their most treasured beliefs merely at the bidding of a few avant-garde thinkers. Yet, if *Essays and Reviews* by no means terminated the influence of Paley's biblical criticism, it did mark the beginning of the end. The heresies of Henry Bristow Wilson, Rowland Williams, Benjamin Jowett, Baden Powell, and Mark Pattison became the orthodoxies of the next generation of English theologians.

Consider the question of miracles. That the Lord Jesus Christ, the Son of God and Savior of mankind, turned water into wine or raised Lazarus from the dead never struck Paley as especially peculiar; in fact, he considered these feats the clinching proof of Christ's authenticity. To a man like Powell, however, the violation of scientific law was ipso facto the credulous fabrication of a primitive mind. "If miracles were in the estimation of a former age among the chief *supports* of Christianity, they are at present the main difficulties and hindrances to its acceptance," the skeptical Powell averred, and he specifically cited Paley as a representative of the outmoded theology.[27] Modernity demanded both a more sophisticated analysis and a different context for argument.

This meant a less literal interpretation of the Scriptures. As a Christian, Benjamin Jowett regarded the Bible as sacred; yet as a classicist steeped in the most advanced techniques of German textual criticism, he maintained that in "the externals of interpretation, that is to say, the meaning of words, the connection of sentences, the settlement of the text, the evidence of facts, the same rules apply to the Old and New Testament as to other books." To Jowett, Paley's biblical criticism suffered from excessive literalism; ignorant of the historical context and too eager to accept each pronouncement as legitimate, Paley had unfortunately concentrated his powers on an ephemeral question. To the modern critic, Jowett wrote, any aspect of revelation that was clearly the product of historical conditioning was no longer tenable and must be abandoned. Though the future master of Balliol supplied regrettably few specific illustrations of his thesis, no sensitive reader missed the point of his essay. In effect, it was the first attempt in England to demythologize the sacred books of the Christian faith.[28]

Essays and Reviews administered yet another blow to the theology of Paley and his admirers; in a brilliant and incisive survey of eighteenth-century British religious thought, Mark Pattison subtly devalued the intellectual credit of his predecessors simply by placing them in historical context. A generally objective observer, Pattison was nevertheless brutal in his ironic tribute to the Paleyan method of biblical research.

> The career of the evidential school, its success and failure—its success in vindicating the ethical part of Christianity and the regulative aspect of revealed truth, its failure in establishing the supernatural and speculative part—have enriched the history of doctrine with a complete refutation of that method as an instrument of theological investigation.[29]

The *Evidences* now became outmoded orthodoxy rather than living proof of the Bible's credibility. To Pattison, as to Jowett and Powell, Paley was as soiled and threadbare as Whately's deists.

Yet, despite their general dissatisfaction with the speculations of their Enlightenment forerunners, the writers of *Essays and Reviews* were, in part, heirs of the eighteenth-century Latitudinarian tradition. Like the Latitudinarians, for example, they emphasized the toleration of new ideas; in his controversial essay "The National Church," Henry Bristow Wilson argued that it was stifling to impose theological uniformity on modern Anglicans, and thus advocated sweeping changes in the Thirty-nine Articles. In a similar manner, Baden Powell averred that "any appeal to argument must imply perfect freedom of conviction."[30] Like the Broad Churchmen of the previous generation, and Paley even before that, the essayists deplored a religion which deliberately shackled inquiry; ideas needed freedom if they were to grow.

It followed that religion had nothing to fear from science—or from Germany. Wilson assured his readers that "if the German Biblical critics have gathered together much evidence, the verdict will have to be pronounced by the sober English judgment." C.W. Goodwin assumed the stance of J. F. W. Herschel's *Preliminary Discourse on the Study of Natural Philosophy* when he warned against attempts to reconcile Genesis and geology. Distinct truths need not clash, he reaffirmed, unless alarmed scientists foolishly tried to juxtapose them. To keep the Bible sacred, it must not be treated as a scientific text.[31]

Finally, virtually all of the essayists believed in a rational, purposeful, and legitimate universe—in a world of design. In the opening pages of the *Essays*, Frederick Temple argued that a meaningless world was "possible to the logical understanding" but not "to the Spirit"; and in publications previous to his contribution to the *Essays*, Powell emphasized strongly the teleological argument; in *The Unity of Worlds and of Nature* he stressed that "the *unity* of science is the reflection of the *unity* of that supreme reason and intelligence which pervades and rules over nature" and in his *Connexion of Natural and Divine Truth* he carefully demonstrated that "the science of nature is but the natural evidence of God."[32] On these matters, the essayists found no quarrel with Paley.

As rational Christians still within the traditions of the eighteenth century, these writers remained open to novel ideas and flexible enough to abandon what no longer could be reasonably justified. If they turned their backs on Paley and the century which produced him, it was not a bitter separation; the essayists built on the foundation of Enlightenment inquiry. And in Cambridge at least, the legacy of Paley's biblical criticism stayed alive and vigorous, as did the central text of the Paleyan system, the *Natural Theology.*

IV

Of Paley's major works, only his *Natural Theology* escaped ruthless criticism in the first half of the nineteenth century. Although discoveries in biology and geology profoundly altered man's view of himself and his past, both the form of Paley's argument and the intellectual principles underlying it attracted scientists and theologians. His major premise that nature everywhere exhibited elements of design was easily adaptable to the changing realities of science. But perhaps equally important was his remarkable lucidity; though he was only one of scores who had employed teleological reasoning in the eighteenth century, his presentation of it stuck tenaciously in the minds of readers long after those of other adherents had faded altogether.

How nineteenth-century scientists seized the argument for their own purposes is a complex issue and one which has proved a rich quarry for many fine scholars.[33] Three aspects of the story deserve further scrutiny: the influence of the *Natural Theology* among Cambridge thinkers who castigated the *Principles;* the forceful reassertion of the argument from design in the Bridgewater Treatises, and the relation of Darwin's discoveries to the concept of *telos* in nature.

The Enlightenment ideal of reconciliation between science and religion was axiomatic among Cambridge scientists of the early nineteenth century. Thus, for example, in a popular manifesto entitled *A Preliminary Discourse on the Study of Natural Philosophy,* J. F. W. Herschel affirmed that science led men away, not from

Christianity, but from prejudice. "The character of the true philosopher is to hope all things not impossible, and to believe all things not unreasonable," he argued; and though he maintained that science must be "independent, unbiassed, and spontaneous," he reasserted the eighteenth-century faith in the "single and consistent" nature of truth.³⁴

It was to this venerable ideal that Adam Sedgwick pledged his science and his philosophy. In the same *Discourse* that castigated the *Principles* for its unforgivable omission of the moral sense, Sedgwick also lavishly praised the *Natural Theology;* it was "impossible," he said, that any writer "or all of them together, should supersede the work of Paley." Though its fundamental argument might be expanded "by new and pregnant illustrations," it could not be radically altered, and thus he strongly recommended "the habitual study of this delightful work."³⁵

As one of the most prominent geologists in England, Sedgwick stood at the center of a series of bitter debates over the origin and structural development of the earth, a topic Paley had neglected but one which had occasionally been discussed during the Enlightenment. In the late eighteenth century, Abraham Gottlob Werner posited that all geological formations were precipitated from water, but this "Neptunist" theory faced almost immediate challenge from James Hutton, whose *Theory of the Earth* (1795) asserted that ancient volcanic eruptions accounted for the deviations in the present structure. Despite heavy criticism, the "vulcanist" theory captured the imagination of a number of scientists and theologians, partly because of its popularization by the talented John Playfair, who maintained that it was more compatible with the argument from design than Werner's theory.³⁶

Then, in 1820, an Oxford geologist, William Buckland, published *Vindiciae Geologiciae,* in which he argued that the earth was formed by a succession of catas-

trophes, including the Mosaic Flood.[37] Though the "cata-
strophic" theory reigned supreme for almost a decade,
it sustained a barrage of telling criticism, culminating
with Charles Lyell's *Principles of Geology,* published
from 1830 to 1833. Marshaling a mass of evidence, Lyell
successfully revived the dormant uniformitarian thesis of
geological development and thereby banished the Flood
from the serious study of the earth. One of Lyell's most
persistent critics, however, was Adam Sedgwick, who ob-
jected vehemently to uniformitarianism because it seemed
to threaten the teleological argument for the existence of
God. "Geology, like every other science when well-inter-
preted, lends its aid to natural religion," he affirmed, thus
placing himself solidly within the tradition of Enlightenment science.[38]

Here was one of the ways, then, in which Paley and
the Enlightenment traditions he summarized exerted a
powerful influence over scientists of the early nineteenth
century, especially those at Cambridge. Although some of
his specific examples may have been outdated—in 1836
Henry Brougham and Charles Bell published a highly
successful edition of *Paley's Natural Theology* in which
they corrected and expanded his illustrations[39]—there
were certain principles, certain assumptions and procedures, intrinsic to Paley and the era he represented which
later scientists and philosophers deeply cherished and
faithfully emulated in their writings.

The first of these principles was that the elements of,
and relationships between, various constituents of the universe were explicable only in terms of the classic rules
of inductive and deductive logic initially enunciated by
Aristotle and thrust in a revolutionary new direction by
Francis Bacon and the "new" scientists of the seventeenth
century. To Paley and his Enlightenment contemporaries,
the world was rationally ordered and therefore subject to
rational inquiry. This meant that nothing of significance

was disallowed from scrutiny, not even the fundamentals of religious belief. Paley devoted one book to proving the existence of God and two more to establishing the credibility of the Gospel, even though he never for a moment doubted either. The purpose of these works, as we have seen, was not to persuade the unbeliever, but to subject God and the Bible to the same kind of dispassionate analysis employed by a scientist when studying, say, the flight of birds or the movement of tides. The enthusiast might assert that God dwelt in his heart, but to the natural theologian such a claim was an imperfect induction; it affirmed only one subjective opinion and lacked objective correlation. It turned its back on reason, the gift of a benevolent Deity.

Second, Paley believed in a purposeful universe, a world animated with Christian meaning and significance. It was not simply that the wing of a butterfly, the necessity of keeping promises, and the suffering of the apostles all embodied a specific religious purpose, a final cause; it was also that these three seemingly disparate phenomena were intimately related to each other by the principle of utility, or expediency, as Paley regrettably put it. The relationship between the intricate anatomical structure of a butterfly's wing and its ability to fly was the same relationship between a kept promise and the happiness of society; it was also the link between the suffering of the apostles and the successful emergence of Christianity in the ancient world. All were useful—and perhaps predestined—means adapted to the benevolent ends of the Almighty Creator. Like many of his predecessors, Paley claimed that there was an intimate connection between the way God structured nature and the manner in which men should conduct their moral and political life. There was also a close relationship between the natural world and the revelations of the Gospel; and these relationships could be discovered by inductive analogy, the acknowledged method of the "new" science. God, man, the Bible, nature, reason, morals, and politics were all linked in Paley's coherent vision of the universe. His was a theology of purposeful relationships, a theology in which a rational observer who employed modern scientific methodology could reveal the ways of God to man.

Third, the world was not only rational and purposeful; it was legitimate as well. Implicit in the teleological argument was the assumption that God never created any phenomenon without a sufficient reason. His purpose may appear mysterious or be obscured by the limited faculties of his favored creatures, but God's universe lacked flaws and blemishes. What followed from this principle proved awkward, but unavoidable. Evil, either natural or moral, was ultimately an illusion since the order of things acquired its legitimacy by the very fact that God had created it. To assert the contrary was to plunge into contradiction.

This legitimacy conferred by the Divine Creator on the natural world extended analogically to the social and political order. In his analysis of nature, the teleologist looked first to the specific physical structure of a plant or animal, and only then determined its purpose or final cause. Thus when the time came to analyze the structure of politics and society, it was only natural that most rational theologians should be heavily biased toward a justification of the status quo. The structure of an institution provided its rationale; and the rationale vindicated its existence. Few teleologists were radicals, fewer still democrats.

These principles were not unique to Paley; they reflected and underscored an ideological consensus among many British intellectuals in the Enlightenment. To the scientist, theologian, moralist, and political economist, the procedures and arguments of natural religion synthesized the scientific and philosophic aspirations of the entire age. Though within this broad consensus disagreements flourished over such specific issues as the existence of a moral sense and the certainty of a priori reasoning, few influential thinkers of the British Enlightenment deviated from the metaphysical assumptions and methodological procedures which united them all.

It was these principles and this consensus that nineteenth century scientists and philosophers fought vigorously to maintain. Any discovery which threatened to undermine the rationality, purposefulness, and legitimacy of the universe immediately aroused the wrath of indignant critics, as Lyell discovered in the 1830s and Darwin thirty years later. Perpetually confronted by alarming discoveries in biology and geology, Sedgwick, Buckland, and other scientists struggled to hold together the alliance of science and religion originally forged in the Enlightenment. Sometimes adjustments had to be made, as in the late 1830s when the Mosaic Flood was quietly abandoned; sometimes the skirmishes were prolonged and bitter, as with the controversy surrounding Robert Chamber's early statement of the evolutionary theory, *Vestiges of Creation,* in the mid-1840s. But there were also instances when all the old assumptions, all the trusted procedures, sprang to life in a single book or series of volumes which asserted the principles that Paley so lucidly summarized in his *Natural Theology.*

Such was the case of the Bridgewater Treatises, commissioned in 1825 by the last will and testament of Francis Henry Egerton, 8th Earl of Bridgewater. In eight treatises by different and often famous authors, "the Power, Wisdom, and Goodness of God as Manifested in Creation" was the dictated theme for one of the most extensive summaries of scientific knowledge in the nineteenth century. John Kidd revealed *The Adaptation of External Nature to the Physical Condition of Man* in treatise two; Peter Mark Roget probed *Animal and Vegetable Physiology* in treatise five; *Chemistry, Meterology, and the Function of Digestion* commanded William Prout's attention in treatise eight.[40] But it was three other treatises which exemplified best the persistence of Paleyan thinking in the mid-nineteenth century.

One of these was William Buckland's *Geology and Minerology Considered with Reference to Natural Theology*, a massive two-volume study that disappointed many observers because it had been expected to refute Lyell's *Principles*. Instead, Buckland merely expanded the argument of his *Vindiciae Geologiciae* sixteen years earlier. Constantly acknowledging his debt to Paley, he again attempted to prove geology "a potent and consistent auxiliary" to both natural and revealed religion. In the eighth chapter, Buckland faced squarely the problem of the killer instinct in animals, an instinct which "may at first sight seem inconsistent with the dispensation of a creation founded in benevolence, and tending to produce the greatest amount of enjoyment to the greatest number of individuals." The solution to this puzzle was both simple and optimistic; sudden death ensured that "the feeble and disabled are speedily relieved from suffering and the world is at all times crowded with myriads of sentient and happy beings." In this manner life itself became a "period of uninterrupted gratification, a scene of continued feasting," and evil, only the temporary illusion of a myopic observer.[41] In Buckland's universe, even the death of a lesser animal had to be legitimized.

In *Astronomy and General Physics*, William Whewell unveiled a universe "of mutual fitness, of conspiring means, of preparation and completion, of purpose and provision." In book one, he discovered the hand of God in such terrestrial adaptations as the length of the year and the variety of climates; in book two, he expanded his analysis to "Cosmical Arrangements" such as the stability of the solar system and the regularity of mechanical laws. In book three, the usually sober-minded Whewell openly marveled at the "whole analogy of creation" and "the manner in which all parts of the universe, the corporeal and intellectual, the animal and moral, are connected with each other." Yet if, as Whewell surmised, "the world of reason and of morality is part of the same creation as the world of matter and of sense," what specific ethical injunctions did men induce from nature's order?[42] On this question Whewell drifted into the shadows; it was not his assignment and had already been answered in the first Bridgewater Treatise of Thomas Chalmers.

Thomas Chalmers's two volumes sought to discover "the marks of divine intelligence in the mechanism of human society."[43] By including man and society in the Deity's grand plan, Chalmers was once again asserting the analogy between nature and morals upon which Paley had founded his utilitarian system. As an Evangelical, however, Chalmers rejected such ethics, affirming in their place the supremacy of conscience. Thus on the one hand, he accepted the basic analogy of Enlightenment morals, while on the other hand he rejected its clear implication.

Although Chalmers was an Evangelical, he was also a Scot who as a student and later a professor of moral philosophy at St. Andrews had read thoroughly the works of the Scottish Common Sense school and knew personally the foremost transmitter of Reid's philosophy, Dugald Stewart.[44] Like many of his Scottish predecessors, Stewart connected the natural and the moral world analogically, but shied away from utilitarianism. Though utility had been "so strongly recommended to some by the powerful genius of Hume, and to others by the well-merited popularity of Paley, . . ." it would lead "to the perpetration of enormities" if adopted by the common people. Since no one could trust "such a fallible and short-sighted creature as Man" to regulate himself by the principle of expediency, only an "internal monitor" could mitigate the difficult problems of ethics.[45] Stewart thus placed himself firmly in the tradition of Hutcheson, Smith, Reid, and other Scottish philosophers who invoked teleological reasoning to establish the moral sense.

Drawing on both his Evangelical and Scottish backgrounds, Thomas Chalmers could therefore assert confidently that "Man is not a utilitarian in his propensities or his principles." Yet it was precisely at this point that Chalmers found the analogy of nature most convenient; as with Malthus and Paley, it became a powerful lever for justifying the existing social and political structure. Rebellion against the class society became fruitless because it violated God's will; private property was "a provision not of man but of God" and "the best scheme for augmenting the wealth of society"; the Poor Laws did "violence to the natural and original distribution of land, and loosened the secure hold of each separate owner on the position which belongs to him." The poor were a "dissipated crew" whose destitution was "the inevitable result of their general worthlessness." No man intrinsically deserved food and shelter since "Nature does not connect this right with existence."[46]

Chalmers's method of argument and his specific conclusions thus represented a confluence of several traditions, including Evangelicalism, the Scottish Common Sense school, Paleyan natural theology, and Malthusian economics. Since to varying degrees each of these schools supported a teleological view of nature and an ethic which buttressed private property and the class society, none of Chalmers's conclusions shocked his contemporaries; his first treatise neatly synthesized almost a century of social thought, and once again demonstrated that Paley's vision of a coherent, consistent universe survived long after the archdeacon had descended to his grave.

The Bridgewater Treatises were thus a focal point of Paley's influence and the kind of thinking he represented, since his most fundamental convictions found sympathy and reinforcement there. The world was rational, and no scientist need fear prying into its most intimate secrets; the world was also purposeful, and in twelve volumes of enormous detail, eight distinguished authors contributed thousands of additional illustrations to confirm this belief. Finally, the world was legitimate; in treatise six Buckland refuted the existence of natural evil, and in the first treatise Chalmers proved the seeming inequities of civil society to be in perfect accordance with nature and with providence.

These assumptions and conclusions persisted long after the Bridgewater Treatises lay shelved and forgotten. In 1850, for example, the irrepressible Adam Sedgwick added a new four-hundred-page introduction to the fifth edition of his *Discourse*. Now the target was not Lyell's *Principles* but Robert Chambers's *Vestiges of Creation*, a highly controversial and ultimately discredited attempt to posit an evolutionary origin of man. Against this heresy Sedgwick championed the trusted orthodoxies; "a unity of plan reigns through all nature," he again insisted, "for we believe that every law, natural and moral, is ordained and upheld by a prescient, all powerful, and unchangeable God." As J. F. W. Herschel had argued twenty years before in his *Preliminary Discourse*, Sedgwick now repeated that "truths, though distinct, are not therefore in conflict," and consequently that "religion had much to hope and nothing to fear from the progress of physical discovery."[47] The Enlightenment consensus was maintained, its assumptions intact; the arguments of Paley's *Natural Theology* lived in the pages of Adam Sedgwick.

Yet, the teleological approach to nature would suffer a fatal blow from another Cambridge man, weaned on the early science of the obstinate Sedgwick and his venerable colleagues. "In order to pass the B.A. examination, it was also necessary to get up Paley's *Evidences of Christianity* and his *Moral Philosophy*," Charles Darwin once wrote in reference to his undergraduate days.

This was done in a thorough manner, and I am convinced that I could have written out the whole of the *Evidences* with perfect correctness. . . . The logic of this book and, as I may add of his *Natural Theology,* gave me as much delight as did Euclid. The careful study of these works, without attempting to learn any part by rote, was the only part of the Academical Course which, as I then felt and as I still believe, was of the least use to me in the education of my mind.[48]

Darwin had entered Christ's—the college of Paley—in January 1828, and there met influential members of the Cambridge intellectual community who encouraged his scientific pursuits and provided him with the working set of methods and assumptions that launched him on his extraordinary career. He met Whewell and accompanied Sedgwick on a geological expedition in 1831. He often called on the mathematician Charles Babbage "and regularly attended his famous evening parties." His first reading of Herschel's *Preliminary Discourse* "stirred up" in him "a burning zeal to add even the most humble contribution to the noble structure of Natural Science." Darwin thus sprang from the same Cambridge soil that nurtured the reputation of Paley's theology through six decades of furious scientific controversy. It consequently comes as no surprise to learn that at one point Darwin "hardly ever admired a book more than Paley's 'Natural Theology' " or that when the *Origin of Species* first appeared, one of its most virulent critics was Adam Sedgwick, the defender of teleology.[49]

The intellectual revolution triggered by Darwin's *Origin of Species* eventually spelled defeat for the Paleyan scheme of a watchmaker Deity, though it by no means routed the teleological argument itself from either scientific or religious thinking. Whereas Paley's argument assumed a fundamentally static universe whose creation had been the single act of an enormously wise and powerful

Creator, Darwin substituted an ongoing process which accounted for the various functions of natural phenomena by the specific exigencies of a particular place and time. In essence, he provided an empirically verifiable alternate to the minor premise of the teleological argument, thereby casting all the prominence and prestige of biology behind Philo's "carelessly" skeptical argument on evolution in Hume's *Dialogues*.[50] Like the term "gravity" in the Enlightenment, "natural selection" became an admittedly abstract, but eminently useful expression that summed up a recognizably scientific phenomenon. The human eye was no longer the gift of God.

What was irrevocably lost in 1859 was the analogue of the watch, the cornerstone of the *Natural Theology* and ultimately of all of Paley's philosophy. The analogue had already been qualified in the Brougham and Bell edition of Paley which appeared in 1836,[51] but it can be argued that it was only with the publication of the *Origin of Species* that the organic conception of nature finally triumphed over the mechanical view that dominated the Enlightenment. The opening six chapters of the archdeacon's final work thus lost much of their relevance and often became little more than a classroom exercise for student novices.

Yet, Paley's coherent vision of a rational, purposeful, and legitimate universe was not completely scuttled by Darwin and his disciples. First, the *Origin* was a triumph of the inductive method; it succeeded where *Vestiges of Creation* had failed because it provided an explanatory mechanism for evolutionary development substantiated by a vast quantity of empirical proof. Certainly Darwin did not accept the static and mechanistic order initially implanted in the Enlightenment mind by the exciting seventeenth-century discoveries in astronomy and physics; for Darwin, the organic realm followed different rules. However, contrary to what both many modern observers and his Victorian contemporaries believed, the

Origin was not an elaborate treatise dedicated to the proposition that chance, not logic, ruled the world. The central Enlightenment assumption that like effects proceeded from like causes was critical for Darwin's biology; without it, he could not have made any valid statements about past developments, and his entire scientific investigation would have collapsed. The crucial weakness of the *Origin*, in fact, lay in its failure to specify the scientific rules for hereditary transformation, a task that Mendel brilliantly accomplished.

Moreover, although Darwin eliminated the Aristotelean final cause and thereby liberated biology from what Bacon and Galileo considered the abiding tyranny of Peripatetic science, the *Origin* was not fundamentally an antiteleological document. What finally separated Darwin from the other biologists of his era was precisely his interest in questions of purpose; why does any species become extinct? why do species vary from one time and place to another? why do we still have an appendix?[52] These are teleological problems which, upon reflection, render nonsensical the famous distinction between "How?" and "Why?" that supposedly separated modern science from its medieval predecessor.

Thus, paradoxically enough, two major aspects of Paley's influence during the nineteenth century manifested themselves in Darwin and the Darwinian revolution. First, Paley was essentially a Cambridge phenomenon; it was at Cambridge that his works dominated the curriculum and there that his admirers and critics arose. Simeon, Coleridge, Sedgwick, Whewell, and Darwin all took their degrees when Paley was an important requirement. For all of them, Paley's works and the traditions they summarized marked the starting point of their own intellectual development. It is difficult to imagine that either Coleridge or Sedgwick would have been so bitterly critical of the *Principles* had they not themselves been subjected to it at an impressionable age. Conversely, the enthusiasm of Sedgwick and Darwin for the *Evidences* and *Natural Theology* would not have been possible had Paley been, like Richard Hey and Daniel Waterland, just another Enlightenment divine on the shelves of a college library. Even Paley's most impassioned adversaries such as William Hazlitt, who read him at Oxford, praised his lucid prose and his systematic argumentation. On style, few disputed that Paley was a perfect choice for an undergraduate text.[53]

Second, though at some point in the nineteenth century each of Paley's works sustained a barrage of incisive criticism, his overall vision of a universe made rational, meaningful, and legitimate by a benevolent Creator survived deep into the nineteenth century. Thus, if it was acknowledged that *Natural Theology* failed to incorporate an adequate conception of time and history, it was also admitted that no philosopher better explicated the teleological argument than Archdeacon Paley. Sedgwick claimed that his own geological investigations merely supplied new examples of Paley's thesis and Darwin continued to admire the work even after the publication of *Origin of Species*. Moreover, though the influx of German biblical criticism meant that some Christians relegated the *Evidences* to a past era of scholarship, these same Christians retained the archdeacon's faith in a rational religion and his scorn for emotive and dogmatic interpretations of Scripture. The Broad Church movement was in the tradition of Locke's *Reasonableness of Christianity; Essays and Reviews* drew strength from many of the same Latitudinarian arguments that encouraged Paley. Finally, the almost universal repudiation of the doctrine of expediency did not extend to the Paleyan link between nature and ethics, between God's design in the external world and his moral dictates to humanity. If Paley formed no distinct school of disciples, his methods and assumptions became a valuable legacy to his successors in the nineteenth century.

V

What, then, were the defining characteristics of Paley's mind? This study has emphasized the unity and cohesiveness of his thought, his insistence on rationality without compromising the deep emotional commitment that lies at the core of traditional Christianity, and his remarkable ability to express himself clearly and forcefully without sacrificing the richness and complexity of his subject matter. Each of these factors played a critical role in shaping the contours of a philosophic system that fused abstract principles and practical knowledge into a synthesis embodying the boldest aspirations and most treasured assumptions of the Enlightenment in Britain. Perhaps, as Coleridge suggested, Paley lacked the insight to penetrate into the depths of man's spiritual life, but he did possess another, equally valuable talent: the ability to summarize and articulate the thoughts and attitudes of thousands of his countrymen on topics ranging from the miracle stories to legal contracts.

For Paley believed that philosophy was a public matter, composed for public consumption. His work gained wide circulation because on important issues he was neither a stuffy nor a pedantic writer, just as he was not a pompous or pretentious man. His self-effacing wit delighted his friends; his undergraduate teaching inspired his students; his lucid prose impressed even his most vehement detractors. Paley's bold excursions into the most fundamental questions of human existence had a freshness and vitality unmatched by most of his contemporaries.

Certainly there are times when Paley becomes downright irritating to the modern reader and loses our sympathy—when he advocates the death penalty for the stealing of sheep, for example, or justifies the corruptions of the English church by appealing to his doctrine of expediency. Nevertheless, he was rarely sophistical or intellectually dishonest. He knew how to weld a mass of amorphous detail into a solid, coherent argument, and he was an outstanding, sometimes brilliant expositor of complex ideas. Paley was a shrewd judge of human nature and his writings have the integrity of one who knows his own mind and does not fear to speak it.

PREFACE

1. William Paley, *The Works of William Paley, D.D.*, ed. Edmund Paley, 7 vols. (London, 1825), 5:xix.
2. John Maynard Keynes, *Essays in Biography* (London: Macmillan & Co., 1933), p. 108n.
3. Ibid.
4. Quoted in Lytton Strachey, *Eminent Victorians* (1918; rpt. New York: Capricorn, 1963), p. 4.
5. Paley, *Works*, 5:xix.

CHAPTER 1

1. Leslie Stephen, *History of English Thought in the Eighteenth Century*, 2 vols. (1876; rpt. New York: Harcourt, Brace & World, Harbinger Book, 1962), 1:346. For the best modern discussions of Paley's life in relationship to his thought, see Ernest Barker, *Traditions of Civility* (Cambridge: Cambridge University Press, 1948), pp. 193–262; and M. L. Clarke, *Paley: Evidences for the Man* (London: SPCK, 1974).
2. George Wilson Meadley, *Memoirs of William Paley, D.D.* (Sunderland, 1809); see also 2d ed. (Edinburgh, 1810); Paley, *Works*, vol. 1.
3. Meadley, *Memoirs*, pp. 1–7; Paley, *Works*, 1:15–24.
4. Paley, *Works*, 1:20–25; Meadley, *Memoirs*, p. 5.
5. Paley, *Works*, 1:28–29; Meadley, *Memoirs*, p. 10.
6. Henry Digby Best, *Personal and Literary Memorials* (London, 1829), pp. 162–64, 182, 193, 214.
7. Paley, *Works*, 4:72.
8. Best, *Memorials*, p. 209.
9. Meadley, *Memoirs*, p. 5.

10. For a list and description of Cambridge reading require-
ments, see Christopher Wordsworth, *Scholae Academicae: Some
of the Studies at the English Universities in the Eighteenth
Century* (Cambridge, 1877), pp. 78–81. Wordsworth relates the
story of one tutor at Pembroke Hall in the 1770s who told a
student, "By all means do not neglect your *duodecimals*. I was
Senior Wrangler in 1767 by knowing my duodecimals." For
more information on mathematics at Cambridge, see W. W.
Rouse Ball, *A History of the Study of Mathematics at Cambridge*
(Cambridge, 1889).

11. ". . . the hardy progeny of the *North,* from Cumberland,
Westmoreland, and the remoter parts of Yorkshire, are usually
the profoundest proficients in *Mathematics* and *Philosophy.*"
Quoted in Gilbert Wakefield, *Memoirs of the Life of Gilbert
Wakefield, B.A.,* 2 vols. (London, 1804), 1:83. See also G. M.
Trevelyan, *Trinity College: An Historical Sketch* (Cambridge:
Cambridge University Press, 1943), p. 88; and Ben Ross
Schneider, *Wordsworth's Cambridge Education* (London: Cam-
bridge University Press, 1957), p. 4.

12. See Charles Henry Cooper, *Annals of Cambridge,* 5 vols.
(Cambridge, 1852), 4:350 ff.; J. Bass Mullinger, *A History of the
University of Cambridge* (London, 1888), pp. 183 ff.; and
Christopher Wordsworth, *Social Life at the English Universities
in the Eighteenth Century* (Cambridge, 1874).

13. Meadley, *Memoirs,* pp. 16–17; Paley, *Works,* 1:38–40.

14. Wordsworth, *Scholae Academicae,* p. 43. Whewell
thought the logic was "such as would make Aristotle stare, and
the Latin would make every classical hair in your head stand on
end."

15. Paley, *Works,* 1:40–41; Richard Watson, *Anecdotes of the
Life of Richard Watson, Bishop of Llandaff,* 2 vols. (London,
1817), 1:19–32.

16. Paley, *Works,* 1:42.

17. Wordsworth, *Scholae Academicae,* pp. 47–48. John
Frere, the other third-year man, had been expected to beat
Paley. Edmund Paley casts doubt on the story (*Works,* 1:39),
which seems to have originated in an article, "Archdeacon
Paley," *Public Characters* 5 (1802–1803): 101–2.

18. Best, *Memorials,* p. 168.

19. Paley, *Works*, 1:63.

20. Ibid., pp. 50, 53.

21. D. A. Winstanley, *Unreformed Cambridge: A Study of Certain Aspects of the University in the Eighteenth Century* (Cambridge: Cambridge University Press, 1935), p. 261. For a listing of Paley's various official posts, see Clarke, *Paley*, p. 13.

22. Quoted in Frida Knight, *University Rebel: The Life of William Frend, 1757–1841* (London: Victor Gollancz, 1971), p. 25. Another description of Paley as a teacher can be found in *Monthly Magazine* 3 (May 1797): 360–61. A list of the books he taught is in his *Works*, 1:129.

23. Brit. Mus. Add. MSS 12,079 and 12,080. The former are Paley's notes on moral and political thought and are partly reproduced in Paley, *Works*, 1:142–61. The latter is his Greek Testament with interleaved notations. The extracts in *Works*, 1:376–428 are not found in the British Museum.

24. Compare, for example, Brit. Mus. Add. MSS 12,079, fols. 1–11 and 52–60, with Paley, *Works*, 4:1–71, 221–24. See also *Works*, 1:138–39.

25. Brit. Mus. Add. MSS 12,079, fols. 8, 43.

26. A list of members is found in Paley, *Works*, 1:68; and a slightly different one in Wakefield, *Memoirs*, 1:132.

27. James Boswell, *Life of Johnson*, ed. George B. Hill and L. F. Powell, 6 vols. (Oxford: Clarendon Press, 1934), 3:416; Paley, *Works*, 1:85–88.

28. Meadley, *Memoirs*, p. 32. Law became master of Peterhouse in 1764 and Casuistical professor ten years later. For an interesting description of him, see *The Diary of the Reverend William Jones, 1777–1821*, ed. O. F. Christie (London: Brentano, 1929), p. 92.

29. Law to Newcastle, 10 November 1756, Brit. Mus. Add. MSS 32,869, fol. 159. See also Law to Hardwicke, 22 November 1756, Brit. Mus. Add. MSS 35,604, fol. 421.

30. Law to Newcastle, 16 May 1760, Brit. Mus. Add. MSS 32,906, fol. 104. Nevertheless, Law was confirmed.

31. William Talbot to Newcastle, 13 November 1764, Brit. Mus. Add. MSS 32,960, fol. 409.

32. John Jebb, *The Works, Theological, Medical, Political and Miscellaneous of John Jebb*, ed. John Disney, 3 vols. (London,

1787), 1:1–27, 117; see also Wordsworth, *Social Life*, p. 334; and George Dyer, *History of the University and Colleges of Cambridge*, 2 vols. (London, 1814), 1:124.

33. Jebb, *Works*, 1:45–52.

34. Watson, *Anecdotes*, 1:25, 17–33.

35. Jebb, *Works*, 1:49–51, 2:319; George Dyer, *The Privileges of the University of Cambridge*, 2 vols. (London, 1824), 2 (Supplement): 110–11, 257.

36. Jebb, *Works*, 2:320–33; Winstanley, *Unreformed Cambridge*, pp. 316–27.

37. Stephen, *History*, 1:343.

38. John Hey, *Lectures in Divinity*, 4 vols. (Cambridge, 1796), 1:8–9, 119; Edmund Law, *Considerations on the Theory of Religion* [1745], 5th ed. (Cambridge, 1764); Jebb, *Works*, 2:83 ff.

39. Law, *Considerations*, p. 251n; Richard Watson, *A Collection of Theological Tracts*, 6 vols. (Cambridge, 1785), 1:ix.

40. Richard Watson, *An Apology for Christianity, in a Series of Letters Addressed to Edward Gibbon, Esquire* (Cambridge, 1776), p. 2.

41. Quoted in W. D. Killen, *The Ecclesiastical History of Ireland*, 2 vols. (London, 1875), 2:336.

42. William Samuel Powell, *Discourses on Various Subjects* (London, 1776), pp. 22–42; Francis Blackburne, *The Works, Theological and Miscellaneous, of Francis Blackburne, M. A.*, 7 vols. (Cambridge, 1805), 1:xxvii–xxx.

43. Francis Blackburne, *The Confessional; or, A Full and Free Inquiry into the Right, Utility, Edification and Success of Established Systematical Confessions of Faith and Doctrine in Protestant Churches* (London, 1766), pp. 20–21.

44. Between 1766 and 1772, over forty pamphlets debated the issues. For what appears to be a complete list of these, see *Gentleman's Magazine* 42 (June 1772):263–65. For more background to the controversy, see also Caroline Robbins, *The Eighteenth Century Commonwealthman* (Cambridge, Mass.: Harvard University Press, 1961), pp. 324–35.

45. Thomas Rutherforth, *A Vindication of the Right of Protestant Churches to Require the Clergy to Subscribe to an Established Confession of Faith and Doctrines* (Cambridge,

1766), p. 4; [Benjamin Dawson], *An Examination of Dr. Rutherforth's Argument respecting the Right of Protestant Churches to Require the Clergy to Subscribe to an Established Confession of Faith and Doctrines* (London, 1766); Thomas Rutherforth, *A Second Vindication of the Right of Protestant Churches to Require the Clergy to Subscribe to an Established Confession of Faith and Doctrine in a Letter to the Examiner of the First* (Cambridge, 1766); *Animadversions upon the Conduct of the Rev. Dr. Rutherforth, in the Controversy Which Has Followed the Publication of the Confessional* (London, 1768), pp. 10–11.

46. Jebb, *Works*, 1:31–33; 3:16–33.

47. Quoted in Norman Sykes, *Church and State in England in the Eighteenth Century* (Cambridge: Cambridge University Press, 1934), p. 383.

48. Winstanley, *Unreformed Cambridge*, p. 312. The reason for the rejections was "that the University had no power of making so material a change, and that the times were not favorable to so great an undertaking." See Dyer, *Privileges*, 2:109.

49. Meadley, *Memoirs*, 2d ed., p. 89.

50. Edmund Law, *Considerations on the Propriety of Requiring a Subscription to Articles of Faith* (Cambridge, 1774), p. 16; Thomas Randolph, *An Answer to a Pamphlet, Entituled* [sic] *Considerations of the Propriety of Requiring a Subscription to Articles of Faith* (Oxford, 1774).

51. Paley, *Works*, 3:293.

52. William Hazlitt, *The Complete Works of William Hazlitt*, ed. P. P. Howe, 21 vols. (London: J. M. Dent, 1930–34), 7:252.

53. See Meadley, *Memoirs*, pp. 115–17.

54. Compare Thomas Rutherforth, *Institutes of Natural Law*, 2 vols. (Cambridge, 1754), 1:334–71, 180–87; 2:37; with Paley, *Works*, 4:21–24, 88–92, 320. Part of the reason for Paley's omission might lie in Rutherforth's personality. One contemporary speaks of "his vanity, which was always ready to overrun" and another criticizes his "authoritative manner." See Brit. Mus. Add. MSS 5810, fol. 83 (Cole MSS); and Hey to Plumptre, 1 December 1812, University Library, Cambridge, Add. MSS 5864, fol. 123.

55. Paley, *Works*, 1:91.

56. "I was told at Durham that it is one of the best parsonages in England," Paley wrote of Bishop-Wearmouth; ". . . the patronage is considerable. . . . The last man got 2000 pounds for one fine." See Paley, *Works*, 1:272–73.

57. Ibid, p. 113.

58. See unnumbered MSS, Giggleswick Grammar School, Giggleswick, Yorkshire.

59. Paley, *Works*, 6:79, 101, 288.

60. Ibid., 1:103; 6:111.

61. Ibid., 6:102, 124; italics eliminated.

62. Ibid., 1:345; Meadley, *Memoirs*, p. 116.

63. Castalia Granville, ed., *Lord Granville Leveson Gower (First Earl Granville) Private Correspondence, 1781–1821*, 2 vols. (London: John Murray, 1916), 2:358; "William Paley," *Gentleman's Magazine*, vol. 75, pt. 2 (July 1805): 675; Henry Gunning, *Reminiscences of the University, Town, and County of Cambridge, from the Year 1780*, 2 vols. (London, 1854), 1:236.

64. Paley, *Works*, 1:341; Meadley, *Memoirs*, p. 195.

65. Paley, *Works*, 1:199; 3:317–31.

66. *A Letter to William Paley, M.A., Archdeacon of Carlisle, from a Poor Labourer, in Answer to His Reasons for Contentment* (London, 1793), p. 2. See also *Letters to William Paley, M.A., Archdeacon of Carlisle, on His Objections to a Reform in the Representation of the Commons* (London, 1796).

67. Paley, *Works*, 4:21; 3:31.

68. Ibid., 2:427; 3:9.

69. Ibid., 1:66. For the best brief discussion of Paley's legalism, see "Religion and Society: Paley and Channing," *National Review*, vol. 6, no. 11 (January 1858): 397–424.

70. Paley, *Works*, 1:272, 291.

71. Porson disliked both Paley's philosophy and his manners. See John Watson Selby, *The Life of Richard Porson, M.A.* (London, 1861), pp. 305–6.

72. Paley, *Works*, 5:xviii. For an account of his final illness, see J. R. Fenwick, *Sketch of the Professional Life of John Clark, M.D.* (Newcastle, 1806), pp. 25–28. See also William Wallace Currie, ed., *Memoir of the Life, Writings, and Correspondence of James Currie, M.D., F.R.S., of Liverpool*, 2 vols. (London,

1831), 1:344 ff.

73. "Natural Theology; or, Evidences of the Existence and Attributes of the Deity," review in *Edinburgh Review*, 5th ed., vol. 1 (January 1803): 287.

CHAPTER 2

1. David Hume, *Hume's Dialogues concerning Natural Religion*, ed. Norman Kemp Smith (Oxford: Clarendon Press, 1935), p. 230.

2. Ibid., p. 38; Peter Gay, *The Enlightenment: An Interpretation*, 2 vols. (New York: Knopf, 1967), 1:417; Stephen, *History*, 1:36.

3. David Hume, *My Own Life*, in *Hume on Religion*, ed. Richard Wollheim (New York: World Publishing Co., Meridian Books, 1964), p. 272.

4. Quoted in E. C. Mossner, *The Life of David Hume* (London: Thomas Nelson & Sons, 1954), pp. 309, 394; *The Letters of David Hume*, ed. J. Y. T. Grieg, 2 vols. (Oxford: Clarendon Press, 1932), 1:323.

5. Yet, the purpose of Hume's philosophy is not always clear. On his intentions, see Norman Kemp Smith, *The Philosophy of David Hume: A Critical Study of Its Origins and Central Doctrines* (1941; rpt. London: Macmillan, Papermac, 1966), esp. pp. 543–66; J. A. Passmore, *Hume's Intentions* (Cambridge: Cambridge University Press, 1952); James Ward Smith, "Concerning Hume's Intentions," *Philosophical Review* 69 (1960): 63–77; V. C. Chappell, ed., *Hume: A Collection of Critical Essays*, (Garden City, N.Y.: Doubleday Anchor, 1966), esp. pp. 6–98.

6. Isaac Newton, *Mathematical Principles of Natural Philosophy and His System of the World*, ed. Florian Cajori from 1729 trans. by Andrew Motte (Berkeley: University of California Press, 1946), p. 400.

7. Charles Coulston Gillispie, *The Edge of Objectivity: An Essay in the History of Scientific Ideas* (Princeton: Princeton University Press, 1961), p. 74.

8. Thomas Sprat, *History of the Royal Society* [1667], ed. Jackson I. Cope and Harold W. Jones (St. Louis: Washington

192   *Notes*

University Studies, 1958), p. 71.

9. Francis Bacon, *The Advancement of Learning* [1605] (London: Oxford University Press, The World's Classics, 1951), p. 103.

10. Galileo Galilei, *Dialogue on the Great World Systems,* ed. Georgio de Santillana (Chicago: University of Chicago Press, 1953), pp. 121–26; Bacon, *Advancement,* p. 113.

11. Robert Boyle, *A Disquisition about the Final Causes of Natural Things* (London, 1688), p. 157. Harvey's own account in his *De motu condis* differs somewhat. See Geoffrey Keynes, *The Life of William Harvey* (Oxford: Clarendon Press, 1966), pp. 26–31. See also Kenneth D. Keele, *William Harvey: The Man, the Physician, and the Scientist* (London: Nelson, 1965), pp. 134–35; and Louis Chauvois, *William Harvey; His Life and Times* (London: Hutchinson Medical Publications, 1957), pp. 181–217.

12. John Ray, *The Wisdom of God Manifested in the Works of the Creation* [1691], 4th ed. (London, 1704), pp. 103, 257.

13. Ibid., p. 17; see also Charles E. Raven, *English Naturalists from Neckam to Ray: A Study of the Making of the Modern World* (Cambridge: Cambridge University Press, 1947); and his *John Ray, Naturalist: His Life and Works* (Cambridge: Cambridge University Press, 1942).

14. See E. A. Burtt, *The Metaphysical Foundations of Modern Physical Science* (1932; rpt. Garden City, N.Y.: Doubleday Anchor, 1957), pp. 207–302; Alexandre Koyré, *From the Closed World to the Infinite Universe* (Baltimore: Johns Hopkins Press, 1957), pp. 155 ff.; Alexandre Koyré, *Newtonian Studies* (1965; rpt. Chicago: University of Chicago Press, Phoenix Books, 1968); A. Rupert Hall, *The Scientific Revolution, 1500–1800: The Formation of the Modern Scientific Attitude,* 2d ed. (1962; rpt. Boston: Beacon Press, 1966), pp. 244–76. The literature on Newton is large, and increasing.

15. Isaac Newton, *Four Letters from Sir Isaac Newton to Dr. Bentley Containing Some Arguments in Proof of a Deity* (London, 1756), p. 1.

16. Colin Maclaurin, *An Account of Sir Isaac Newton's Philosophical Discoveries* [1748], 3d ed. (London, 1775), p. 33.

17. Newton, *Mathematical Principles,* p. 398.

18. Henry More, *An Antidote against Atheism* [1653], in *The Cambridge Platonists*, ed. C. A. Patrides (Cambridge, Mass.: Harvard University Press, 1970), p. 237. On More, see Aharon Lichtenstein, *Henry More: The Rational Theology of a Cambridge Platonist* (Cambridge, Mass.: Harvard University Press, 1962).

19. Ralph Cudworth, *The True Intellectual System of the Universe* [1678], trans. John Harrison, 3 vols. (London, 1845), 1:348.

20. Sprat, *History*, p. 348; Browne quoted in Raven, *Naturalists*, p. 343.

21. Matthew Tindal, *Christianity as Old as the Creation; or, the Gospel, a Republication of the Religion of Nature* [1730], 2d ed. (London, 1732), p. 89.

22. On deism, the best general work remains the ancient but venerable Gotthard Victor Lechler, *Geschichte Des Englischen Deismus* (Stuttgart and Tübingen, 1841). Two useful studies of English deists are James O'Higgens, *Anthony Collins: The Man and His Works* (The Hague: Martinus Nijhoff, 1970), and Cecilia Motzo Dentice di Accadia, *Preilluminismo e Deismo in Inghilterra* (Naples: Libreria Scientifica Editrice, 1970), which, despite the ambitious title, is actually on Blount.

23. Newton, *Mathematical Principles*, p. 398.

24. For the best brief discussion of Lord Herbert of Cherbury, see Basil Willey, *The Seventeenth Century Background: Studies in the Thought of the Age in Relation to Poetry and Religion* (1934; rpt. Garden City, N.Y.: Doubleday Anchor, 1953), pp. 127–37; John Locke, *The Reasonableness of Christianity* [1695], ed. I. T. Ramsey (Stanford: Stanford University Press, 1967), p. 32.

25. Maclaurin, *Account of Newton*, p. 95; or, as Robert Boyle put it, science was "the handmaid to divinity." See *The Works of the Honourable Robert Boyle*, 6 vols. (London, 1772), 4:3.

26. See the excellent edition of *The Leibniz-Clarke Correspondence*, ed. H. G. Alexander (Manchester: Manchester University Press, 1956).

27. See Bertrand Russell, *A Critical Exposition of the Philosophy of Leibniz* (1900; rpt. London: George Allen and Unwin, 1937), esp. chaps. 2 and 3.

28. Gottfried Wilhelm Leibniz, *New Essays concerning Human Understanding*, trans. A. G. Langley (New York, 1896), p. 22; see also pp. 64–85.

29. James Gibson, *Locke's Theory of Knowledge and Its Historical Relations* (1917; rpt. Cambridge: Cambridge University Press, 1968), pp. 267–309.

30. John Herman Randall, *The Career of Philosophy*, 2 vols. (New York: Columbia University Press, 1962), 1:50–76. See also Walther Arnsperger, *Christian Wolff's Verhältnis zu Leibniz* (Weimar, 1897).

31. R. R. Palmer, *Catholics and Unbelievers in Eighteenth Century France* (1939; rpt. New York: Cooper Square, 1961), p. 17 and passim.

32. This is not to suggest that the philosophes ignored metaphysics. See, for example, Ira O. Wade, *The Intellectual Development of Voltaire* (Princeton: Princeton University Press, 1969), esp. p. 573 ff.; and Thomas L. Hankins, *Jean d'Alembert: Science and the Enlightenment* (Oxford: Clarendon Press, 1970).

33. Ray quoted in Aram Vartanian, *Diderot and Descartes: A Study of Scientific Naturalism in the Enlightenment* (Princeton: Princeton University Press, 1953), p. 68; Voltaire, *Philosophical Dictionary* [1769], trans. and ed. Peter Gay, 2 vols. (New York: Basic Books, 1962), 1:271.

34. Vartanian, *Diderot*, pp. 98, 201 ff.

35. Hume, *Dialogues*, p. 204.

36. Hume, *Letters*, 1:187; David Hume, *Enquiries concerning the Human Understanding and concerning the Principles of Morals*, ed. L. A. Selby-Bigge from 1777 ed., 2d ed. (1902; rpt. Oxford: Clarendon Press, 1966), p. 44.

37. David Hume, *A Treatise of Human Nature* [1739], ed. L. A. Selby-Bigge (1888; rpt. Oxford: Clarendon Press, 1968), p. 89, italics eliminated; Hume, *Enquiries*, p. 49; Kemp Smith *Philosophy of Hume*, pp. 23–51.

38. Hume, *Enquiries*, p. 72.

39. Hume, *Dialogues*, p. 178.

40. Hume, *Letters*, 1:155.

41. Hume, *Dialogues*, pp. 192, 280.

42. David Hume, *The Natural History of Religion* [1757], ed.

H. E. Root (Stanford: Stanford University Press, 1957), pp. 27, 42–43.

43. Hume, *Dialogues*, pp. 239–45.

44. For Hume's arguments on "natural evil," see *Dialogues*, pp. 25–58.

45. Ibid., p. 162.

46 Chappell, *Hume: Critical Essays*, esp. pp. 129–86; Randall, *Career*, 1:635–50; Kemp Smith, *Philosophy of Hume*, pt. 3.

47. On the Common Sense school, see Andrew Seth Pringle-Pattison, *Scottish Philosophy: A Comparison of the Scottish and German Answers to Hume*, 3d ed. (Edinburgh: W. Blackwood & Sons, 1899); Henry Laurie, *Scottish Philosophy in Its Natural Development* (Glasgow: J. Maclehose & Sons, 1902); and Selwyn A. Grave, *The Scottish Philosophy of Common Sense* (Oxford: Clarendon Press, 1960). For a particularly interesting contemporary critique, see Joseph Priestley, *An Examination of Dr. Reid's Inquiry into the Human Mind on the Principles of Common Sense* (London, 1774). Priestley argues that Reid and his disciples radically misinterpreted the epistemology of both Descartes and the English empiricists.

48. Thomas Reid, *An Inquiry into the Human Mind on the Principles of Common Sense* [1764], 2d ed. (Edinburgh, 1765), pp. v–vii, 17ff.

49. James Beattie, *An Essay on the Nature and Immutability of Truth in Opposition to Sophistry and Scepticism* [1770], 4th ed. (Edinburgh, 1773), pp. 50, 476–78.

50. James Oswald, *An Appeal to Common Sense in Behalf of Religion*, 2 vols. (Edinburgh, 1772), 1:98.

51. Beattie, *Essay*, pp. 367–68.

52. Blaise Pascal, *Pensées*, trans. John Warrington from 2d ed. of Louis Lafuma (1953; rpt. London: Dent, Everyman's Library, 1960), pp. 2, 96.

53. Leland quoted in Mossner, *Life of Hume*, p. 291; William Warburton, *The Works of the Right Reverend William Warburton, D.D., Lord Bishop of Gloucester*, ed. Richard Hurd, 12 vols. (London, 1811), 12:341.

54. Hume, *Letters*, 2:311.

55. Hume, *Dialogues*, p. 281, italics eliminated.

CHAPTER 3

1. Percy Bysshe Shelley, *Shelley's Prometheus Unbound: A Variorum Edition*, ed. Lawrence John Zillman (Seattle: University of Washington Press, 1959), p. 126.

2. See David Hume, *Essays*, ed. T. H. Green and T. H. Grosse, 2 vols. (London, 1875), 1:144–50.

3. Quoted in G. R. Cragg, *From Puritanism to the Age of Reason* (Cambridge: Cambridge University Press, 1966), p. 40n; George Berkeley, *The Works of George Berkeley, Bishop of Cloyne*, ed. A. A. Luce and T. E. Jessop, 9 vols. (London: Nelson, 1950), 8:144.

4. Quoted in Roland Stromberg, *Religious Liberalism in Eighteenth Century England* (Oxford: Oxford University Press, 1954), p. 9.

5. Paley, *Works*, 7:405–44.

6. John Ray, *The Wisdom of God Manifested in the Works of the Creation* [1691], 4th ed. (London, 1704); William Derham, *Physico-Theology; or, A Demonstration of the Being and Attributes of God from His Works of Creation* [1713], 3d ed. (London, 1714); and William Derham, *Astro-Theology; or, A Demonstration of the Being and Attributes of God from a Survey of the Heavens* [1715], 3d ed. (London, 1719).

7. Paley, *Works*, 5:1–2. Hereafter in this chapter, all page references to Paley's *Natural Theology* (vol. 5 of the *Works*) will be placed in parentheses in the text.

8. Cicero, *De natura Deorum*, trans., H. Rackham (Cambridge, Mass.: Harvard University Press, Loeb Classical Library, 1956), pp. 217, 219.

9. Marie Boas Hall, ed., *Robert Boyle on Natural Philosophy: An Essay with Selections from His Writings* (Bloomington: Indiana University Press, 1965), pp. 57 ff.

10. Bernard Nieuwentyt, *The Religious Philosopher; or, The Right Use of Contemplating the Works of the Creator*, trans. John Chamberlayne, 3 vols. (London, 1719), 1:xlvi–xlvii.

11. Joseph Butler, *The Works of Bishop Butler*, ed. J. H. Bernard, 2 vols. (London: Macmillan, 1900), 2:2–5.

12. See Thomas Franklin Mayo, *Epicurus in England, 1650–1725* (Dallas: Southwest Press, 1934); and Samuel I. Mintz, *The Hunting of Leviathan: Seventeenth Century Reactions*

to the Materialism and Moral Philosophy of Thomas Hobbes
(Cambridge: Cambridge University Press, 1962), pp. 66–79.

13. Hume, *Dialogues,* pp. 207–8.

14. William Paley, *Natural Theology: Selections,* ed. Frederick Ferre (Indianapolis: Bobbs-Merrill, Library of Liberal Arts, 1963), p. xxiii.

15. Loren Eiseley, *Darwin's Century: Evolution and the Men Who Discovered It* (1958; rpt. Garden City, N.Y.: Anchor Books, 1961), pp. 27–55.

16. See, for example, Susanne K. Langer, *Philosophy in a New Key: A Study of the Symbolism of Reason, Rite, and Art* (1942; rpt. New York: Mentor Books, 1960), p. 15.

17. A list of the works Paley consulted can be found in his *Works,* 1:321.

18. William Cheselden, *The Anatomy of the Human Body* [1713], 7th ed. (London, 1750), p. 334.

19. Derham, *Physico-Theology,* "To the Reader," n.p.; pp. 86 ff., 183 ff.

20. Paley, *Works,* 1:320.

21. Ibid., 7:38.

22. Ibid., 1:30, 248–49. Carlyle considered himself something of a poet; see his *Poems, Suggested Chiefly by Scenes in Asia Minor, Syria and Greece* (London, 1805).

23. John Clive, *Scotch Reviewers: "The Edinburgh Review," 1802–1815* (London: Faber & Faber, 1957), p. 149.

24. *Leibniz-Clarke Correspondence,* pp. 15–20.

25. Alfred North Whitehead, *Science and the Modern World* (1925; rpt. New York: Mentor Books, n.d.), pp. 41–56.

26. For a discussion of the controversy, see Basil Willey, *The Eighteenth Century Background: Studies on the Idea of Nature in the Thought of the Period* (1940; rpt. Boston: Beacon Press, 1961), pp. 43–56.

27 Alexander Pope, *An Essay on Man,* Epistle 1, lines 233–94. See also Arthur O. Lovejoy, *The Great Chain of Being: A Study of the History of an Idea* (1936; rpt. New York: Harper Torchbooks, 1960), pp. 183–207.

28. Frederick Ferre, *Language, Logic and God* (1962; rpt. London: Collins, Fontana Library of Theology and Philosophy, 1970), pp. 103–16.

29. Isaac Barrow, *The Theological Works of Isaac Barrow* (Oxford, 1830), 4:427.

30. Boyle, *Works*, 4:22.

31. For some interesting examples, see Marjorie Hope Nicolson, *Newton Demands the Muse: Newton's Opticks and the Eighteenth Century Poets* (1946; rpt. Princeton: Princeton University Press, 1966), pp. 37–38.

32. Newton, *Mathematical Principles*, p. 546; William King, *Divine Predestination and Foreknowledge Consistent with the Freedom of Man's Will* (Dublin, 1710), p. 4; Peter Browne, *The Procedure, Extent, and Limits of Human Understanding* [1728], 3d ed. (London, 1737), p. 83.

CHAPTER 4

1. Thomas Woolston, *A Discourse on the Miracles of Our Saviour, in View of the Present Controversy between Infidels and Apostates* [1727], 5th ed. (London, 1728), pp. 4–5.

2. Samuel Clarke, *A Discourse concerning the Unchangeable Obligations of Natural Religion, and the Truth and Certainty of the Christian Revelation* [1705], 4th ed. (London, 1716), pp. 294–95, 301.

3. Butler, *Works*, 2:222–23.

4. Ibid., 2:239.

5. Hume, *Enquiries*, pp. 114–19, 127.

6. Two of the most thoughtful attacks were John Douglas, *The Criterion; or, Rules by Which the True Miracles Recorded in the New Testament Are Distinguished from the Spurious Miracles of Pagans and Papists* [1752] (London, 1807); and George Campbell, *A Dissertation on Miracles: Containing an Examination of the Principles Advanced by David Hume, Esq.; in an Essay on Miracles* (Edinburgh, 1762).

7. Hume, *Enquiries*, p. 114.

8. Paley, *Works*, 2:4. Hereafter in this chapter, all page references to the *Evidences* (vol. 2 of *Works*) will be identified by the abbreviation *E* and cited in parentheses in the text. Page references to *Horae Paulinae* (vol. 3 of the *Works*) will be identified by the abbreviation *HP* and will also be cited in parentheses in the text.

9. Campbell, *Dissertation*, p. 48.

10. Hume, *Enquiries*, p. 116.

11. Stephen, *History*, 1:354.

12. See George Gilbert, *Interpretation of the Bible: A Short History* (New York: Macmillan Co., 1908), pp. 224–59; Robert M. Grant, *A Short History of the Interpretation of the Bible* (London: Adam and Charles Black, 1965), pp. 111–22; and Luigi Salvatorelli, "From Locke to Reitzenstein: The Historical Investigation of the Origins of Christianity," *Harvard Theological Review*, vol. 22, no. 4 (October 1929): 263–80.

13. Samuel Clarke, *A Paraphrase of the Four Evangelists*, 2 vols. (London, 1714), 1:iv; John Locke, *The Works of John Locke*, ed. Edmund Law, 8th ed., 4 vols. (London, 1777), 1:285.

14. Nathaniel Lardner, *The Works of Nathaniel Lardner, D.D.*, ed. Andrew Kippis, 11 vols. (London, 1788), vol. 2, pt. 1, p. 3.

15. Paley's choice of title for the book was probably inspired by such works as John Lightfoot, *Horae Hebraicae et Talmudicae* (Cambridge, 1658), and Isaac Watts, *Horae Lyricae* (London, 1706). For a brief discussion of the title, see *Gentleman's Magazine*, vol. 78, pt. 1 (February 1808): 104.

16. Hume, *Enquiries*, pp. 110–11, 116.

17. Ibid., p. 121.

18. Stephen, *History*, 1:157–230.

19. Hume, *Enquiries*, pp. 117, 119, 121.

20. Paley, *Works*, 1:189.

CHAPTER 5

1. Paley, *Works*, 4:xii, x, xiii. Hereafter in this chapter all page references to Paley's *The Principles of Moral and Political Philosophy* (vol. 4 of *Works*) will be placed in parentheses in the text.

2. Paley, *Works*, 5:349; 7:132.

3. See, for example, Stephen, *History*, 2:89–90.

4. Daniel Walker Howe, *The Unitarian Conscience: Harvard Moral Philosophy, 1805–1861* (Cambridge, Mass.: Harvard University Press, 1970), p. 67.

5. Compare Rutherforth, *Institutes of Natural Law*, 1:146–

59, 322-73, 474-88; with the conclusions in Paley, *Works*, 4:59-64.

6. *Oxford English Dictionary* (1933), *s.v.* "expediency."

7. Stephen, *History*, 2:89-105; Ernest Albee, *A History of Utilitarianism* (London: Swan Sonnenschein, 1902), pp.70, 161, 166, 201; John Plamenatz, *The English Utilitarians* (Oxford: Basil Blackwell, 1958), p. 51. Plamenatz makes Paley a disciple of Hobbes as well.

8. Stephen, *History*, 2:74-102.

9. See above, n. 5, and Chapter 1.

10. See, for example, Stanley Grean, *Shaftesbury's Philosophy of Religion and Ethics: A Study in Enthusiasm* (Athens, Ohio: Ohio University Press, 1967); and Willey, *Eighteenth Century Background*, pp. 57-75.

11. Earl of Shaftesbury [Anthony Ashley Cooper], *Characteristics of Men, Manners, Opinions, Times* [1711], 5th ed., 3 vols. (London, 1732), 2:15.

12. Ibid., p. 16.

13. Ibid., pp. 89-90.

14. Francis Hutcheson, *A System of Moral Philosophy*, 2 vols. (London, 1755), 1:1.

15. Ibid., p. 51.

16. Ibid., pp. 38, 97. See also pp. 53-79, 175.

17. Ibid., pp. 177-79.

18. Adam Smith, *The Theory of Moral Sentiments* [1759], 4th ed. (London, 1774), pp. 237-38, 169, 185.

19. Ibid., p. 189.

20. Quoted in Willey, *Eighteenth Century Background*, p. 85.

21. Butler, *Works*, 2:46.

22. Ibid., pp. 4, 7.

23. Paley, *Works*, 1:341.

24. Mark 10:23.

25. R. R. Palmer, *The Age of the Democratic Revolution: A Political History of Europe and America, 1760-1800*, 2 vols. (Princeton: Princeton University Press, 1959).

26. Thus, for example, in a lengthy oration advocating toleration of Roman Catholics delivered in the House of Commons in 1805, Charles James Fox deemed Paley an authority "which all

who love profound learning, exalted virtue, and sound morals, must respect." He then proceeded to quote him extensively. See *Cobbett's Parliamentary Debates, during the Third Session of the Second Parliament of the United Kingdom of Great Britain and Ireland* (London, 1805), 4:846 ff.

27. See, in particular, M. J. C. Vile, *Constitutionalism and the Separation of Powers* (Oxford: Clarendon Press, 1967), esp. pp. 98–118; and W. B. Gwyn, *The Meaning of the Separation of Powers: An Analysis of the Doctrine from Its Origins to the Adoption of the United States Constitution* (New Orleans: Tulane University Press, 1965).

28. Ernest Barker, *Traditions of Civility* (Cambridge: Cambridge University Press, 1948), pp. 246–54.

29. David Hume, *Essays: Moral, Political, and Literary* [1741–42] (Oxford: Oxford University Press, 1963), p. 45.

30. Vile, *Constitutionalism*, pp. 106–7.

31. Barker, *Traditions*, p. 245.

32. Leon Radzinowicz, *A History of English Criminal Law And Its Administration from 1750*, 4 vols. (London: Stevens & Sons, 1948), 1:301–449. See also Sir William Holdsworth, *A History of English Law*, 12 vols. (London: Methuen & Co., 1938), 11:274–80.

33. "I saw crimes of the most pernicious nature pass unheeded by the law," Bentham recalled in horror on one occasion, "acts of no importance put in point of punishment upon a level with the most baneful crimes; punishments inflicted without measure and without choice." Quoted in Mary P. Mack, *Jeremy Bentham: An Odyssey of Ideas, 1748–1792* (London: Heineman, 1962), p.66.

34. Radzinowicz, *History*, 1:257.

35. For the best analysis of Warburton's discussion, see Norman Sykes, *Church and State in England in the Eighteenth Century* (Cambridge: Cambridge University Press, 1934), pp. 316–26.

36. Paley, *Works*, 7:94–95, 97.

37. For Bentham's reaction to Paley, see Jeremy Bentham, *The Works of Jeremy Bentham*, ed. John Bowring, 11 vols. (Edinburgh, 1843), 10:163–65.

CHAPTER 6

1. Clarke, *Paley*, p. 129.

2. Quoted in D. A. Winstanley, *Early Victorian Cambridge* (Cambridge: Cambridge University Press, 1940), p. 151.

3. Thomas Coward, *An Analysis of Paley's Moral and Political Philosophy* . . ., 2d ed. (Cambridge, 1842), pp. 190–91.

4. Richard Whately, ed., *Paley's Moral Philosophy: With Annotations* (London, 1859), p. iii.

5. Thomas Gisborne, *The Principles of Moral Philosophy Investigated, and Briefly Applied to the Constitution of Civil Society* (London, 1789), pp. 33–34, 200.

6. Paley's *Principles* was defended in George Croft, *A Short Commentary with Strictures, on Certain Parts of the Moral Writings of Dr. Paley and Mr. Gisborne* (Birmingham, 1797), but attacked in Thomas Green, *An Examination of the Leading Principle of the New System of Morals* (London, 1799); Thomas Ludlam, *Six Essays upon Theological, to Which Are Added Two upon Moral Subjects* (London, 1798); and Peter Roberts, *Observations on the Principles of Christian Morality and the Apostolic Character* (London, 1796).

7. Quoted in Robert Isaac and Samuel Wilberforce, *The Life of William Wilberforce*, 5 vols. (London, 1838), 2:351.

8. Samuel Taylor Coleridge, *The Complete Works of Samuel Taylor Coleridge*, ed. W. G. T. Shedd, 7 vols. (New York, 1884), 1:158, 193n, 263; 2:296.

9. On the Evangelical reaction to natural religion, see, for example, William Wilberforce, *A Practical View of the Prevailing Religious System of Professed Christians* . . . (London, 1797), pp. 7–19; John Overton, *The True Churchman Ascertained; or, An Apology for Those of the Regular Clergy Who Are Sometimes Called Evangelical Ministers* . . . [1801], 2d ed. (York, 1802), passim; and Isaac Milner, *Sermons, by the Late Very Reverend Isaac Milner*, 2 vols. (London, 1820), 1:5–45; 2:392–447.

10. "Disgrace" quoted in Herschel Baker, *William Hazlitt* (Cambridge, Mass.: Harvard University Press, Belknap Press, 1962), p. 14; William Hazlitt, *The Complete Works of William Hazlitt*, ed. P. P. Howe, 21 vols. (London: J. M. Dent & Sons,

1930–34), 7:200, 252. For the reaction of another Romantic to Paley, see Shelley's "Refutation of Deism: A Dialogue," in which one of the participants, Eusebes, invokes the major arguments of both Paley's *Evidences* and his *Natural Theology*, only to have them shattered by the quick wit and precocious logic of the skeptic Theosophus. See Percy Bysshe Shelley, *The Complete Works of Percy Bysshe Shelley*, ed. Roger Ingpen and Walter Peck, 10 vols. (London: Ernest Benn, Julian Editions, 1928), 6:27–45.

11. Winstanley, *Early Victorian Cambridge*, p. 18.

12. Edward Pearson, *Remarks on the Theory of Morals* ... (Ipswich, 1800), pp. 70–77, 144; Latham Wainewright, *A Vindication of Dr. Paley's Theory of Morals* ... (London, 1830).

13. One scholar has called this group "the Cambridge Network." See Walter F. Cannon, "Scientists and Broad Churchmen: An Early Victorian Intellectual Network," *Journal of British Studies*, vol. 4, no. 1 (November 1964): 65–88. See also Robert Robson, "Trinity College in the Age of Peel," in *Ideas and Institutions of Victorian Britain: Essays in Honour of George Kitson Clark*, ed. Robert Robson (London: G. Bell & Sons, 1967), pp. 312–36.

14. See John Willis Clark, *The Life and Letters of the Reverend Adam Sedgwick*, 2 vols. (Cambridge, 1890), 1: passim.

15. Adam Sedgwick, *A Discourse on the Studies of the University* (Cambridge, 1833), pp. vi, 49, 54, 57.

16. William Whewell, *On the Foundations of Morals* (Cambridge, [1837]), p. vii; William Whewell, *The Elements of Morality, including Polity*, 2 vols. (London, 1845), 1:368.

17. John Stuart Mill, *Dissertations and Discussions: Political, Philosophical, and Historical*, 4 vols. (London, 1859), 1:127. The original articles were somewhat revised for this collection of essays.

18. Ibid., pp. 124, 146, 151–52, 158.

19. Ibid., 2:454–58, 485–86.

20. Thomas Coward, *An Analysis of Paley's Evidences of Christianity, with Examination Questions to Each Chapter, and a Copious Collection of Senate-House Examination Papers, with References for Answers* (Cambridge, 1836). Two other examples are Charles H. Crosse, *An Analysis of Paley's Evidences* ...

(Cambridge, 1855); and J. M. Bacon, *A Short Analysis of Paley's Evidences* . . . (Cambridge, 1870). Many other titles can be found in the British Museum catalogue, although a number of the pamphlets themselves were destroyed by bombing during the Blitz.

21. J. P. Taylor, *A Consideration of Some Recent Strictures on Paley's Evidences of Christianity* (Cambridge, 1898), p. 2.

22. "Paley's Ghost," *Paley Verses* (Cambridge, 1909), p. 19.

23. J. J. Blunt, *Undesigned Coincidences in the Writings Both of the Old and New Testament* [1827] (London, 1847); William Van Mildert, *An Inquiry into the General Principles of Scripture Interpretation* (Oxford, 1815); Henry Hart Milman, *The Character and Conduct of the Apostles Considered as an Evidence of Christianity* (Oxford, 1827).

24. Whately, *Paley's Moral Philosophy*, pp. 23–31; Richard Whately, ed., *A View of the Evidences of Christianity*, (London, 1859), pp. 2, 4–5.

25. Richard Whately, *Christian Evidences: Intended Chiefly for the Young* (London, n.d.), p. 23.

26. For recent discussions of the book, see Owen Chadwick, *The Victorian Church*, 2 vols. (London: Adam and Charles Black, 1966, 1970), 2:75–86; and M. A. Crowther, *Church Embattled: Religious Controversy in Mid-Victorian England* (London: Archon, 1970). See also Charles R. Sanders, *Coleridge and the Broad Church Movement* (Durham, N.C.: Duke University Press, 1942).

27. Baden Powell, "On the Study of the Evidences of Christianity," in *Essays and Reviews* (London, 1860), p. 129.

28. Benjamin Jowett, "On the Interpretation of Scripture," in ibid., p. 337 and passim. On Jowett and the controversy that followed the publication of his essay, see Geoffrey Faber, *Jowett: A Portrait with Background* (Cambridge, Mass.: Harvard University Press, 1958), pp. 229–88.

29. Mark Pattison, "Tendencies of Religious Thought in England, 1688–1750," in *Essays and Reviews*, p. 297.

30. Henry Bristow Wilson, "Séances historiques de Genève: The National Church," in ibid., pp. 200–235; Powell, "Evidences," p. 96.

31. Wilson, "Séances," p. 151; C. W. Goodwin, "On the Mosaic Cosmogony," in *Essays and Reviews*, pp. 25–53.

32. Frederick Temple, "The Education of the World," in *Essays and Reviews*, p. 1; Baden Powell, *The Unity of Worlds and of Nature: Three Essays* (London, 1856), pp. 84–85; Baden Powell, *The Connexion of Natural and Divine Truth; or, The Study of the Inductive Philosophy Considered as Subsequent to Theology* (London, 1838), p. 203.

33. One of the best studies of this episode in intellectual history remains Charles Coulston Gillispie, *Genesis and Geology: A Study in the Relations of Scientific Thought, Natural Theology, and Social Opinion in Great Britain, 1790–1850* (1951; rpt. New York: Harper Torchbooks, 1959).

34. J. F. W. Herschel, *A Preliminary Discourse on the Study of Natural Philosophy* (London, 1830), pp. 1–4.

35. Sedgwick, *Discourse*, p. 88.

36. Gillispie, *Genesis*, pp. 41–76.

37. William Buckland, *Vindiciae Geologiciae; or, The Connection of Geology with Religion Explained* (Oxford, 1820).

38. Quoted in Gillispie, *Genesis*, p. 147.

39. Henry Brougham and Charles Bell, eds., *Paley's Natural Theology, with Illustrative Notes*, 2 vols. (London, 1836), vols. 1 and 2.

40. John Kidd, *On the Adaptation of External Nature to the Physical Condition of Man, Principally with Reference to the Supply of His Wants, and the Exercise of His Intellectual Faculties*, Bridgewater Treatise no. 2 (London, 1833); Peter Mark Roget, *Animal and Vegetable Physiology Considered with Reference to Natural Theology*, Bridgewater Treatise no. 5, 2 vols., (London, 1834); William Prout, *Chemistry, Meteorology and the Function of Digestion Considered with Reference to Natural Theology*, Bridgewater Treatise no. 8 (London, 1834).

41. William Buckland, *Geology and Mineralogy Considered with Reference to Natural Theology*, Bridgewater Treatise no. 6, 2 vols. (London, 1836), 1:9, 129–31.

42. William Whewell, *Astronomy and General Physics Considered with Reference to Natural Theology*, Bridgewater Treatise no. 3 (London, 1833), pp. 17, 230, 255.

43. Thomas Chalmers, *On the Power, Wisdom, and Goodness of God as Manifested in the Adaption of External Nature to the Moral and Intellectual Constitution of Man,* Bridgewater Treatise no. 1, 2 vols. (London, 1833), 1:6.

44. See Daniel F. Rice, "Natural Theology and the Scottish Philosophy in the Thought of Thomas Chalmers," *Scottish Journal of Theology,* vol. 24, no. 1 (February 1971): 23–46.

45. Dugald Stewart, *The Collected Works of Dugald Stewart,* ed. William Hamilton, 11 vols. (Edinburgh, 1854), 2:354–55.

46. Chalmers, *Power,* 2:65; 1:238, 252; 2:9, 12, 27, 50.

47. Adam Sedgwick, *A Discourse on the Studies of the University of Cambridge,* 5th ed. (London, 1850), pp. cxlvii, cclvii, cccxxi.

48. Charles Darwin, *The Autobiography of Charles Darwin, 1809–1882,* ed. Nora Barlow (London: Collins, 1958), p.59.

49. Ibid., pp. 66–69, 108; Francis Darwin, ed., *The Life and Letters of Charles Darwin,* 3 vols. (London, 1887), 2:219. On Sedgwick's criticism of Darwin, see Stephen Toulmin and June Goodfield, *The Discovery of Time* (London: Hutchinson & Co., 1965), pp. 224–25.

50. See Philo's speech on an evolutionary explanation for the development of nature in Hume, *Dialogues,* p. 215.

51. Brougham and Bell, *Paley's Natural Theology,* p. 1n.

52. Gertrude Himmelfarb, *Darwin and the Darwinian Revolution* (1959; rpt. Garden City: Doubleday & Co., Anchor Books, 1962), pp. 157–59.

53. Thomas De Quincey recounts the story of how, as a student at Oxford, his tutor assigned Paley, explaining, "Ah! an author excellent for his matter, only you must be on your guard as to his style; his is very vicious *there.*" De Quincey disagreed; he argued that Paley's "homey, racy, vernacular English" had "never been attained in a degree so eminent." It was his philosophy that was "a jest, the disgrace of the age." See Thomas De Quincey, *The Collected Writings of Thomas De Quincey,* ed. David Masson, 14 vols. (Edinburgh, 1889), 2:62.

ALTHOUGH THE NOTES INDICATE THE RANGE OF PRIMARY sources and secondary material which I have consulted in preparing this study, a few comments on materials specifically relating to Paley might be useful.

Of the numerous editions of Paley published in the nineteenth century, the best remains *The Works of William Paley, D. D.*, edited by Edmund Paley, 7 vols. (London, 1825), which went through a second edition in 1838. Edmund Paley devotes the first volume to a discursive but valuable biography of his father, which should be supplemented by the two editions of George Wilson Meadley, *Memoirs of William Paley, D.D.* (Sunderland, 1809); 2d ed. (Edinburgh, 1810). Meadley is particularly informative on Paley's years at Cambridge. In his *Personal and Literary Memorials* (London, 1829), Henry Digby Best offers the most vivid account of Paley as a conversationalist.

Less remains of Paley's personal papers than might be expected. Extracts of his lecture notes can be found in both the British Museum and at Christ's College, Cambridge. The grammar school at Giggleswick, Yorkshire, has a number of Paley's sermons, most of which were eventually published. Paley wrote few letters, his son informs us, and of those that remain, some of the most interesting can be found in the Keynes Manuscript Collection, Kings College, Cambridge. Other letters are contained in the Additional Manuscripts (Miscellaneous), British Museum; Additional Manuscripts, University Library, Cambridge; English Literature Manuscripts, Boston Public Library; Laing Manuscripts, Edinburgh University Library; Manuscript Collection, National Library of Scotland; and the Montague Manuscripts, Bodleian Library, Oxford. The will of Paley is in the Public Record Office, London.

M. L. Clarke's *Paley: Evidences for the Man* (London: SPCK; Toronto: University of Toronto Press, 1974) appeared when my own manuscript was already in the final stages of preparation. I believe our works complement each other nicely. As his title suggests, Professor Clarke devotes considerably more attention to Paley's life, and, for the most part, treats his work chronologically rather than thematically, as I have done. I have also concentrated much more heavily on the intellectual background of Paley's thought and on his influence in the nineteenth century. Finally, among the other remarkably few modern treatments of Paley, the best remains Ernest Barker, "Paley and His Political Philosophy," *Traditions of Civility* (Cambridge: Cambridge University Press, 1948), pp. 193–262. I have benefited much from this pioneering essay.